The
Scots-Irish
in the
Carolinas

D1452801

by

BILLY KENNEDY

Causeway PRESS

AMBASSADOR PRODUCTIONS

The Scots-Irish in the Carolinas
© 1997 Billy Kennedy

First published September, 1997

THE SCOTS-IRISH CHRONICLES

Scots-Irish in the Hills of Tennessee
Scots-Irish in the Shenandoah Valley
Scots-Irish in the Carolinas

PRINTED IN NORTHERN IRELAND

Published by

Causeway Press

Ambassador Productions Ltd.,
Providence House
16 Hillview Avenue,
Belfast, BT5 6JR

Emerald House Group Inc.
1 Chick Springs Road, Suite 206
Greenville, South Carolina, 29609

About *the Author*

BILLY KENNEDY is assistant editor of the Ulster/Belfast News Letter, Northern Ireland's leading morning newspaper and the oldest English language newspaper, having been founded in 1737. He was born in Belfast in 1943, but has spent almost his entire life living in Co. Armagh. He comes of Scots-Irish Presbyterian roots and has a deep fascination for his forebears of that tradition who moved to America in such large numbers during the 18th century. For the past 25 years, Billy Kennedy has been one of the leading journalists in Northern Ireland, covering the major stories of the Ulster troubles and as a prolific columnist on a variety of issues. He was a news editor with the News Letter for 18 years and in his present capacity as assistant editor of the newspaper, he is the leader writer and is also religious affairs, local government correspondent and literary editor. He is an authority on American country music and culture, travels to Nashville regularly and he has interviewed for the News Letter, personalities such as Garth Brooks, George Jones, Willie Nelson, Charley Pride, Ricky Skaggs, Crystal Gayle, George Hamilton IV, Kenny Rogers and Reba McEntire. For research on his books, 'The Scots-Irish in the Hills of Tennessee', published in 1995; 'The Scots-Irish in the Shenandoah Valley' in 1996; 'The Scots-Irish in the Carolinas', in 1997, he travelled extensively through Virginia, Tennessee, South Carolina and North Carolina and met and talked with many people with direct links to the Scots-Irish settlers of 200 years ago. Billy Kennedy is also a specialist on sport and for 30 years he has written and compiled various publication for soccer internationally and on the local domestic football scene in Northern Ireland. He has been a director for 24 years of Linfield Football Club, Northern Ireland's leading soccer club. He has edited and compiled books on cultural traditions in Ireland, including two on the history of Orangeism in Ireland. He is married with a grown-up daughter.

Dedication

*This book is dedicated to my loving wife Sally,
daughter Julie and my parents.*

Billy Hennesy

*"The wise in heart will be called a discerning man, and
pleasant speech will increase learning."
– Proverbs, chapter 16, verse 21.*

*The author acknowledges the help and support given to him in the
compilation of this book by Samuel Lowry, of Ambassador
Productions, Gregory Campbell of Causeway Press and Tomm
Knutson, of Emerald House. It was again a team effort!*

List *of contents*

Cover Painting: *The American Rifleman*
by H. David Wright, Nashville

The colonial rifleman with his deadly long-rifle is legendary. The same firm resolve that forged these bold frontiersmen, many of them Scots-Irish, into staunch British foes during the Revolutionary War drove the Long Knives to push beyond Blue Ridge to explore and settle a new nation.

• The author acknowledges with thanks, David Wright's gesture in allowing his painting 'The American Rifleman' to be used as the cover for this book.

Thanks

In compiling this book I would gratefully acknowledge the tremendous help and assistance given to me by so many people in the United States. From across the Appalachian region and from other American states I have received a shoal of information on the Scots-Irish families who settled on the frontier 200/250 years ago. I fully appreciate the time and effort taken by those to whom the Scots-Irish tradition and culture means so much and I greatly value the many letters of support sent to me for this project. I hope that through this book, and my previous works 'The Scots-Irish in the Hills of Tennessee', and 'The Scots-Irish in the Shenandoah Valley', many people will come to know and understand the sacrifices made by a strong resolute people in creating a civilisation and a structured way of life in a wilderness. The United States would not be the nation it is today had it not been for the pioneering spirit of the Scots-Irish. Their valour and outstanding achievements make them a special people.

Billy Kennedy

The author can be contacted at:

49 Knockview Drive,
Tandragee,
Craigavon,
Northern Ireland,
BT62 2BH.

Foreword *from the United States*

Dr. John Rice Irwin

Now comes Billy Kennedy with his new book, 'The Scots-Irish in the Carolinas', his third in what might be called a series, or maybe a trilogy, on the great influence the Scots-Irish folk have had on the various regions in America. His first book dealt with the 'Scots-Irish in the Hills of Tennessee', an area largely recognised as having been heavily influenced by that group; and his second book, 'The Scots-Irish in the Shenandoah Valley', addressed the profound contributions of the Scots-Irish in that most beautiful and historic valley of Virginia.

Billy has now turned his attention to the Scots-Irish in North and South Carolina, and the impact and influence which those people have had on the Carolinas and subsequently on American history is most impressive. As in his other books, Billy has used the colorful, heroic, and fascinating individuals to tell the story. What better way is there to explain a culture and convey the meaning of a region than to look into the lives of the individuals who collectively constitute that region's history?

Billy chronicles the lives of Presidents Jackson, Polk, and Johnson, who were born there; and he talks of the other United States Presidents, such as Jimmy Carter and Woodrow Wilson, who had roots in the Carolinas; and he looks at many other Americans of Scots-Irish descent such as John C. Calhoun, who was one of the most influential citizens of his time, and who served as a Congressman, Senator, Secretary of War, Secretary of State, as well as Vice-President under President John Quincy Adams and Andrew Jackson. He talks of "the first Declaration of Independence" from Britain which was drawn and signed in Mecklenburg County, North Carolina, brought about largely through the efforts of Scots-Irish leaders; and he points out the pivotal role which the Scots-Irish played in winning the Revolutionary War. He provides the reader with sketches of many of the important Scots-Irish families of these states, and he examines the contributions they made in virtually every aspect of the early development of the region..

The impact of this volume is important for the revelations which Billy Kennedy makes about the many contributions made by the Scots-Irish in the states of North and South Carolina. It may be of even more importance by titillating others to think, study and examine the cultural and political heritage and legacy of the Scots-Irish. And it may help the citizens of these and other states to develop an awareness of our past, and a thirst to study and learn from our rich history. It may also result in our developing a sense of the history, and of time and place, to better understand the present, and to contemplate the future with renewed insight and wisdom. We may even become as excited and exuberant about our history as our Scots-Irish friend, Billy Kennedy.

Dr. John Rice Irwin
Norris, Tennessee

* **JOHN RICE IRWIN** is founder and director of the Museum of Appalachia in Norris, Tennessee, a farm-village settlement which has gained publicity and acclaim throughout the United States. He is a former college, university and public school teacher and has served as both school principal and county school superintendent. He has also engaged successfully in farming, real estate, Appalachian music (he has his own eight-member string band), and several small businesses and corporations which he started.

John Rice's main interest, however, lies in the people of his native Southern Appalachian Mountains. Since childhood he has spent virtually all his spare time visiting and talking with these mountain folk whom he admires and loves. He is considered to be one of the leading authorities on the history, culture, and people of Southern Appalachia, and on the American pioneer-frontier life in general. John Rice Irwin, born of pioneer ancestors of a Scots-Irish and Welsh lineage, is a prolific author, having written five books on life in the Southern Appalachian region.

The Scots-Irish *(Scotch-Irish) designation*

Scots-Irish is the term used to describe the people who settled in the American frontier in the 100 years from about 1717. Some in the United States today refer to the "Scotch-Irish", but this term now causes offence to many of the Scots-Irish tradition in Britain and America where "Scotch" is looked upon as an alcoholic spirit. In Northern Ireland the designation Ulster-Scot is very widely used by the Presbyterian descendants of the early frontier settlers. Nevertheless, for all the sensitivities it still touches upon, the term "Scotch-Irish" has an historical reality and utility. Ulsterman Francis Mackemie (Makemie), the founding father of the Presbyterian Church in America, was enrolled in the University of Glasgow in February, 1676 as "Franciscus Makemus Scoto-Hyburnus".

The form "Scotch-Irish" would have been used in the vernacular, as "Scotch" was the proper idiom until the 20th century for both language and people. "Scotch-Irish" had been used for the Ulster-Scots in America as early as 1695, but usually in a figurative way. The early Presbyterians from Ireland generally knew themselves simply as "Irish" and were thus known by the other colonists. The later establishment and rapid growth of highly visible and politicised Irish Roman Catholic communities led many Protestants in the United States to adopt the Scotch-Irish label.

Foreword *from Northern Ireland*

Alister J. McReynolds

In this the third instalment of Billy Kennedy's saga of the Scots-Irish in the Appalachian states a number of features emerge which distinguish those who settled in the Carolinas from the folk who set down roots in Virginia and Tennessee. One of the most obvious influences is the impact which proximity to the sea had on the culture and everyday lives of these early pioneers.

Consider in this respect the story of young Johnston Blakely, who was born close to the County Down shore in the little village of Seaforde in October, 1781. His family emigrated to South Carolina and died one by one leaving him orphaned and penniless. In 1800 a friend procured a midshipman's warrant for him and he began a career which led to his involvement with the American navy in the War of 1812-15.

In 1813 he served on The Enterprise and at the beginning of 1814, was promoted to command The Wasp. Soon after, he fell in with the British ship Reindeer in latitude 48° 36' and after an action lasting 20 minutes captured her with an American loss of 21 killed and wounded compared with 67 British casualties. In August 1814 he captured a British merchant ship under convoy and on September 1 the Avon struck her flag to him. Before he could take possession a fresh British ship appeared and Blakely whose ship was somewhat damaged was obliged to sheer off. This was the very last account of him. His ship was spoken of as having been spotted in the Azores and he was thought to have foundered at sea.

In 1816 the legislature of North Carolina, "resolved unanimously, that Captain Blakely's child be educated at the expense of this state, and that Mrs. Blakely be requested to draw on the treasurer of this state from time to time for such sums of money as shall be required for the education of the said child". In this Scots-Irish/Carolina story the pattern is established – a vignette of courage, hardship and gratitude.

Appropriately, Billy Kennedy's portrayal of Andrew Jackson is impressive in substance and style for Jackson is the ultimate icon of the Scots-Irish diaspora. On a personal level I have reason to find Jackson a complex mixture of greatness and violent excess. Perhaps this is due in part to the fact that one of my ancestors on my mother's side – Adam Arbuthnot was personally hanged by Andrew Jackson. Albeit, Arbuthnot was a British officer who had been running arms to the Seminole Indians. Ironically, this is balanced in that the mother of another direct ancestor, General Andrew Thomas McReynolds of Dungannon, County Tyrone and later of Grand Rapids, Michigan, was a full cousin of Andrew Jackson.

Jackson was born 18 months after his parents left County Antrim and his mother was an extraordinary woman who died while attending the American prisoners of war in the prison ship at Charleston. As they say in America Jackson was, "somethin' else", or as McGee put it, "like Sixtus Quintus, Columbus and Cromwell, much reflection upon him does not beget the sense of dimness, but of substantiality. We have blood and bone in every incident of his life and every word he has uttered". Jackson might have died in obscurity as a teenager had it not been for the leniency of fellow Ulsterman Francis Rawdon, heir to the Earl of Moira in County Down, who as a brilliant 25-year-old British commander released back into her care the reckless son of Elizabeth Hutchinson Jackson from imprisonment in Camden.

I like to think that Rawdon did this because he was persuaded by the dignity and distinctive accent of his own native Ulster that was embodied in this fine woman. Doyle gives us an amazing image of the young Jackson, "with piercing blue eyes, face as long as a Lurgan spade, high shock of red hair, and lonely resolution". As Billy Kennedy's portrait adds action to this image, we see how Jackson was to embark on the career of frontier soldier, land speculator and American hero that would lead him to the Presidency by 1828.

Again on the personal side a few years ago I recall a discussion which I had with some American friends in Cherokee, North Carolina after we had watched the open-air play "Unto These Hills". The play depicts Jackson's harsh 'Trail of Tears' treatment of the native Americans. The discussion centred on whether Jackson was a great man on the one hand or a violent despot on the other. We concluded that it was invidious to judge the people and events of the past by the standards of today and that in the final analysis Andrew Jackson was a complex and contradictory mixture of both courage and violent passion. And so, in this persona, Jackson symbolises both the strength and the excess of the Scots-Irish as a people. One thing is for sure, however, and that is the realisation that America would never have evolved into what it is today – the world's superstate had it not been for the early total contribution of both the flaws and strengths of these people, warts 'n' all.

Billy Kennedy's interest in the Scots-Irish roots of contemporary music emerge in this book as in the previous two volumes in the series. In this aspect of cultural evolution the Scots-Irish of the Carolinas were catalytic in the early days before Nashville became the mecca of country music that it is today. Filling the backcountry they brought the Scottish and Irish pentatonic mode which pre-empted the folk music tradition of the entire Appalachian region. Notably in the Carolinas, particularly Ulster forms of imagery and narrative ballads may be traced which had an impact on both the secular and the sacred gospel lyrics which were grafted on to these airs.

What is clear also is that the Carolinas attracted not just the lowliest echelons of Ulster society but also the ranks of the wealthy and significant. The patrician background of the Polk, Calhoun and Dobbs families in Ireland prior to emigration to the Carolinas is well documented.

Above all else this book tells a story not just of a people who brought much with them but also it is a portrayal of able and pragmatic pioneers who quickly learned to adapt to a new and sometimes harsh environment. Robert Witherspoon in his recollections of life in **Colonial South Carolina** spoke of the experience of trying to survive a sea-borne hurricane in a home he built as a mud wall house similar to those of his native Ulster, – "the rain quickly penetrated through the poles and brought down the sand that covered over, which seemed to threaten to cover us alive ..... I believe we all sincerely wished ourselves again at Belfast."

Of course, they weren't again at Belfast and the practical response to disastrous experiences like this led to the adoption and ingenious adaptation of the log cabin into something of their own. After that – the rest as they say – is history.

Alister J. McReynolds, MA, BEd, DASE, DLIS, FRSA,
Principal of Lisburn College of Further and Higher Education,
County Antrim.
July 1997.

SOURCES:
1. **Ireland, Irishmen and Revolutionary America** by D. N. Doyle.
2. **Albion's Seed** by D. H. Fischer.
3. **Irish Settlers in North America** by T. D. McGee.

ALISTER JOHN MCREYNOLDS, a graduate of Stranmillis College (Belfast), Queen's University (Belfast), and the University of Ulster, is a chartered librarian as well as qualified teacher. He is a Fellow of the Royal Society of Arts, with an interest in local history.

1

Northern *Ireland*

Northern Ireland is an integral part of the United Kingdom with a population of 1.6 million. Its geographical boundary takes in six of the nine counties of the Irish province of Ulster. The majority of the people in Northern Ireland, almost two-thirds, are Protestant and British by culture and tradition, and committed to maintaining the constitutional link with the British Crown.

Just over one-third of the population is Roman Catholic, most of whom are Irish by culture and tradition and seek the reunification of Ireland through a link-up with the Irish Republic. A sizeable number of Roman Catholics in Northern Ireland are known to favour maintaining the status quo link with Britain, therefore it is wrong to look at the political breakdown through a strict sectarian headcount.

The one million Protestants in Northern Ireland are descendants of Scottish and English settlers who moved from the British mainland in the 17th and 18th centuries. Presbyterians, who formed the bulk of those who moved to the American frontier lands in the 18th century, are today the most numerous Protestant tradition in Northern Ireland, totalling 400,000. The Church of Ireland (Anglican Episcopal) community account for 350,000 people, Methodists 70,000 with smaller Protestant denominations accounting for the rest.

Belfast (population 500,000) is the capital of Northern Ireland and the six counties are Antrim, Down, Londonderry, Tyrone, Armagh and Fermanagh.

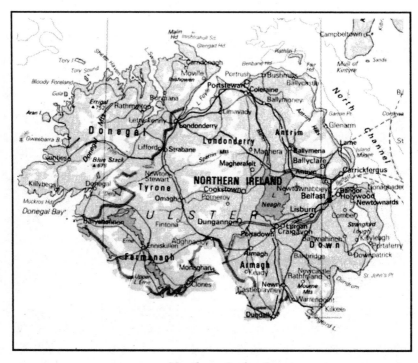

Northern Ireland

2

South *Carolina*

S outh Carolina is a state that epitomises the American south in culture, social life and traditions. Triangular in shape, it is situated at a pivotal point on the Atlantic seaboard, has a northern land border with North Carolina and a south western border with Georgia. The state was one of the earliest of the American colonies, first explored by the Spanish and French in the mid-16th century, and 100 years later by the English, who organised the first permanent settlements.

Topographically, South Carolina consists of two large regions divided by the fall line of waterfalls and river rapids in the territory of the capital city of Columbia (population 100,000). To the north west of this line is the Piedmont Plateau, a region where a large number of Scots-Irish settlers moved in the 18th century. The state reaches the foothills of the Blue Ridge Mountains in this location. To the south west of Columbia the land drops off to the Atlantic Plain, the low country, a region of plantation settlements and a rich agricultural belt.

South Carolina has a population of 3.5 million, largely rural with a white/black ethnic breakdown of 69/30 per cent. One per cent consists of native American Indian, Asian and Hispanics. Outside of Columbia, the other main population centres are Charleston (80,000), North Charleston (70,000), Greenville (65,000), Spartanburg (45,000), Rock Hill (35,000), Florence (30,000), Anderson (30,000), and Greenwood (25,000).

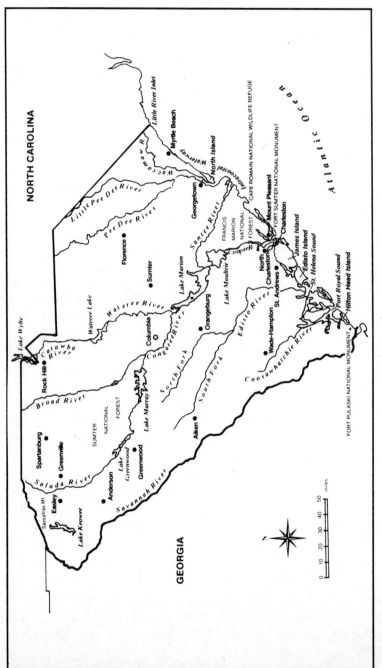

On May 23, 1788, South Carolina became the eighth state to ratify for the Union. It had been one of the 13 original American colonies, but was heavily involved in the vanguard for independence at the time of the Revolutionary War. This came about in the settlements of the Upper Piedmont region by the Scots-Irish, Welsh and German families, who were disaffected by the colonial government based in the "low country" and dominated by wealthy English plantation owners.

The state was also central to the events in the American Civil War of 1861-65. South Carolina's senior statesman and son of an Ulsterman John Caldwell Calhoun was the author of the 'Nullification Doctrine' on states' rights and it was the first state to secede from the Union. The first battle of the war was fought at Fort Sumter, Charleston and the state was a stronghold for the Confederate cause.

The towns of Greenville, Spartanburg, Rock Hill, Anderson, Greenwood and Abbeville emerged partly from Scots-Irish settlements in the 18th century. Indeed, the population of Anderson, close to the Savannah River border line with Georgia, is composed mostly of descendants of Scots-Irish settlers from Virginia and Pennsylvania, who, it was said, moved to the hilly country of South Carolina for summer comfort. The warm climate in Greenville enticed many Scots-Irish families to move from Pennsylvania, while at Spartanburg the population grew up largely from the influx of the Ulster immigrants.

The first white settler in present Greenville county was Irish-born Richard Pearis, who came from Virginia in 1765 as a trader. He married a Cherokee woman and in his association with the native Americans he acquired large tracts of land which today occupy the town of Greenville.

In the early years of South Carolina as a state of the Union government at the capital Columbia life was far from peaceful, as the diverse cultures of the sturdy up-country Scots-Irish and the low country English dandies mixed. There were heated arguments in the State House, fisticuffs and brawls on the streets, and "more gentlemanly" duels in secluded places. The state's legislators set about confronting prejudices by means of education and friendships between young men from the various parts of the state. This manifested itself in the South Carolina College (now university) at Columbia, founded in 1801.

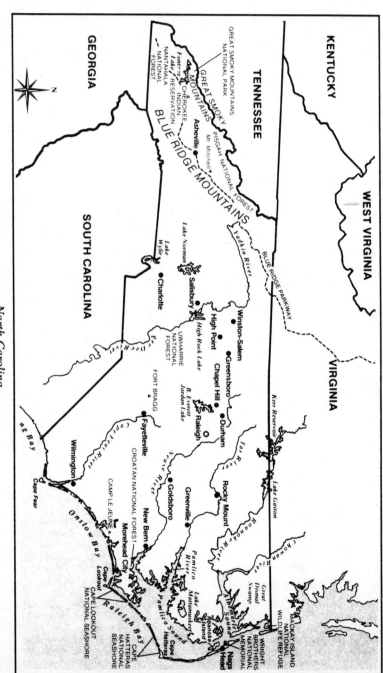

3

North *Carolina*

North Carolina was the site of the first English colony in America, and today it is one of the most populous states in the Union, with a population of six million and a half. The state may have been the birthplace of the first English child born in America, but it was also the first state to declare its readiness for independence from the British Crown. After Texas, North Carolina is the main manufacturing region in the South and it also leads the way in agricultural produce, heavily dependent as it is on the land. There is a distinctive rural ambience in North Carolina, which, before the advent of a more industrialised approach in the latter part of this century, earned it the reputation of being the "Rip Van Winkle State".

North Carolina, like neighbouring Appalachian states, has a high inland mountain range, a central plateau and a low coastal plain. To the north it is bordered by Virginia, to the west by Tennessee along the ridge line of the Great Smoky Mountains, to the south over a 60-mile stretch with Georgia and over 250 miles by South Carolina. North Carolina was discovered by French and Spanish explorers in the early 16th century, but it was the English in the Elizabethan reign who settled the region, through initiatives by Sir Walter Raleigh and Sir Richard Grenville.

The Carolinas existed as one single British colony until 1729 when North Carolina and South Carolina became separate royal dependencies. The region was heavily populated by native American tribes and the seeds of conflict built up when large numbers of Scots-Irish settlers from Virginia moved into the Piedmont Plateau and Blue Ridge mountain lands in the mid to latter part of the 18th century.

The "Regulator Movement" was established among the independent Scots-Irish population who sought to resist unfair taxation on small farmers from the colonial government agencies in the east. The Watauga settlement in the area, which today is North East Tennessee, emerged in the struggle by the Scots-Irish settlers for freedom and the 1775 Mecklenburg Declaration of Independence signed on North Carolina soil was the forerunner for the more significant document signed at Philadelphia a year later.

On April 12, 1776, North Carolina was the first state to declare its independence from Britain and some of the most significant battles of the Revolutionary War were fought in the state. In the American Civil War, a century later, North Carolina was sympathetic to the Confederate cause, but was reluctant to secede largely due to the state constitution which accorded greater representation to the small inland farmers to correct past domination by coastal plantation owners. It was only after Abraham Lincoln's call for troops to rally to the Union flag, that North Carolina found it had no option but to become the final member of the Confederacy. In the Civil War it was estimated that North Carolina lost more men in battle than any other American state.

North Carolina was admitted to the Union on November 21, 1789, the 12th state to ratify the constitution. It was also one of the 13 original British colonies. Of the six million population in North Carolina today, 76 per cent is white and 22 per cent black. Native Americans account for one per cent (mostly Cherokees), and Asians and Hispanics one per cent.

Raleigh, the capital city, has a population of 150,000, but the largest city is Charlotte with 320,000 inhabitants. Other main centres are Greensboro (160,000), Winston Salem (135,000), Durham (100,000), High Point (65,000), Fayetville (60,000), Asheville (55,000), Gastonia (50,000), Wilmington (45,000) and Rocky Mountain (40,000).

The population in North Carolina is highly significant in that 70 per cent of it consists of life-long residents of the state, many who can trace their ancestry back to the first Scots-Irish settlers of the 18th century. Next to Tennessee and Virginia, North Carolina would have the biggest predominance of Scots-Irish families in the United States – the roots of the hardy Presbyterian stock who moved from Ulster 200/250 years ago are deeply embedded here.

BLOOD TIES (A Letter Home)
to the people of Northern Ireland

From lonely green Donegal on the Shamrock shore
my family so long ago came,
to walk in that beautiful homeland no more
nor speak of its magical name.
Deep ties of blood were then left far behind
to slumber across long generations –
to flicker in dreams 'neath a son's restless mind,
the bond to that far-distance nation.

'Cross the high winds of history and the fathomless sea
to the far Pennsylvania coast –
to the south and the west, past the fierce Cherokee,
at the head of a great Celtic host –
to Carolina's highlands my forefathers came,
then pushed on toward wild Tennessee;
the legacy left to me: my family name
and an Ulster-Scot's need to be free.

From the battle-scarred lowlands of bonny Scotland
to the north of the great Emerald Isle,
through the Valley Forge winter to sweet Dixie land,
Celts have struggled for every mile.
Let me never forget that I stand on this ground
because Ulster-Scots could not abide
the yoke of injustice half the world 'round
and would die before a life without pride.

Though long years have passed, with those blood ties near-lost
in the centuries' amnesiac flood,
I remember my freedom was gained at great cost
and that our homelands are stained with one blood.
And that circle unbroken still binds us this hour,
growing stronger with each passing year;
in the fiddles and bagpipes still travels this power:
'tis the memory of kinship we hear.

ROBERT ASHLEY LOGUE
Sumner County, Tennessee, 1997.

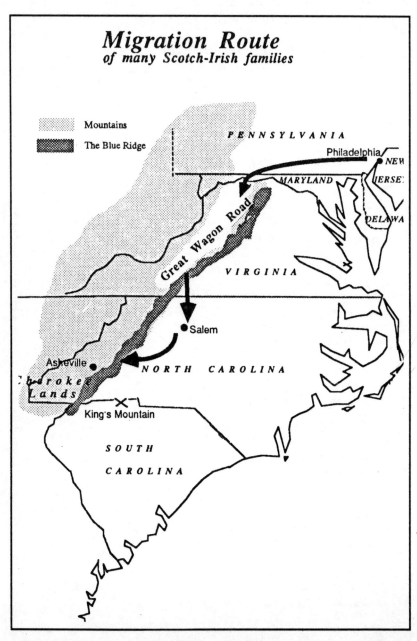

Migration Route
of many Scotch-Irish families

Mountains

The Blue Ridge

PENNSYLVANIA

Philadelphia

NEW

JERSE

MARYLAND

DELAWA

Great Wagon Road

VIRGINIA

Salem

Asheville

NORTH CAROLINA

Cherokee Lands

King's Mountain

SOUTH

CAROLINA

Map shows the main migration route of the Scotch-Irish from Pennsylvania to Western North Carolina

4

Early movement *to America*

The Eagle Wing is believed to have been the first ship to set sail from Ulster's shores to America, but its 1636 voyage from the little Co. Down port of Groomsport was aborted after heavy storms in mid-Atlantic. Some 140 Presbyterians from congregations on both sides of Belfast Lough in North Co. Down and East Co. Antrim sailed from Groomsport on September 9 bound for Boston. The journey ended back in Carrickfergus Bay on November 3 with the ships shrouds asunder, mainsail in ribbons, and rudder badly damaged.

It had been a traumatic experience for the voyagers who had completed three-quarters of the journey when one of the Presbyterian ministers accompanying them, the Rev. John Livingstone advised, in the face of the continuing storm, that it was God's will that they should return home. The ship's captain was also of similar mind and the 150-tonne vessel was turned around.

The Eagle Wing journey, notwithstanding its apparent failure, is remarkable in that it took place only 16 years after the Pilgrim Fathers landed at Plymouth Rock in Pennsylvania after crossing the Atlantic on the Mayflower.

Between 1717 and the American Revolutionary War years of the late 1770s and early 1780s an estimated quarter of a million Scots-Irish Presbyterian settlers left the Province of Ulster in the northern part of Ireland for the new lands across the Atlantic. They travelled in extremely hazardous conditions, in simple wooden sailing ships from the ports of Belfast, Larne, Londonderry, Newry and Portrush for the far-off berths of Philadelphia, New Castle (Delaware), Charleston,

Baltimore and New York. Huddled together with the most meagre of belongings and money, they were a people forced to move because of the severe restrictions placed on their faith by the ruling British establishment of the day, and because of the economic deprivations prevailing in their Ulster homeland.

The first regular Scots-Irish emigrant ships were chartered in 1717 and in that year, when drought completely ruined the crops on the Ulster farmlands, 5,000 men and women headed to Pennsylvania. The first recorded passenger ship was "The Friends Goodwill" which left Larne for Boston in April, 1712. There were five great waves of immigration to America from Ulster in the 18th century: 1717-18, 1725-29, 1740-41, 1754-55 and 1771-75.

Next to the English, the Scots-Irish by the end of the 18th century became the most influential section of the white population in America, which, by 1790, numbered 3,172,444. At that time, the Scots-Irish segment of the population totalled about 14 per cent and this figure was much higher in the Appalachian states of Virginia, Tennessee, Kentucky and North Carolina.

In a very short period, the Ulster-Scots and their off-spring progressed from being immigrant settlers to become naturalised Americans, totally assimilated in the fabric of their new nation. Their involvement in the War of Independence made the Scots-Irish think less of their old country and more of the lush fertile lands that were opening up in front of them. As they pioneered the Carolinas, Virginia, and the new states of Kentucky and Tennessee they were increasingly doing so as Americans, not as Irish or Scots.

The Ulster settlers tended to settle together and mixed little with the English and Germans already there. Poverty also forced them from the more expensive land in the east to the frontier regions, where land was cheap and readily available; others simply squatted in defiance of the authorities. There were, however, drawbacks, none more so than the risk of being attacked by Indians. Colonial officials were glad to have the Ulster people to provide a defence against hostile natives. When trouble arose, the Scots-Irish settlers were left to their own devices, an experience which hardened and embittered them against the British Government, just as had been the case back home in Ulster.

It is generally acknowledged that the Revolutionary War for independence in America in the 1770s was essentially a dispute between the Scots-Irish immigrants and the Crown, especially in the Appalachian region. In some Appalachian states in 1776, the Ulster-Scots population was at least one-third.

From Pennsylvania, the Ulster settlement spread along the Valley of Virginia during the 1730s and 1740s following the Great Philadelphia Wagon Road. This was the famous 'backcountry' where their presence was welcomed as a reinforcement against the Indian threat. Most of the movement into North Carolina took place between 1740 and 1756, with the surge into South Carolina developing in the 1760s. The move into East Tennessee developed about 1770-1780.

By the time the Revolutionary War came, about 90 per cent of the Ulster settlers had made their homes in Pennsylvania, the Valley of Virginia and the Carolinas. The Ulster settlers became quite a formidable force. Abandoned to their fate by their British masters, who had let them down so many times in the past, the Ulstermen and women began to feel themselves American above everything else. Ulster families were in the vanguard of the push west. Moving across the mountain barriers, many would leave Virginia for Kentucky, or North Carolina for Tennessee, while many others migrated from eastern Pennsylvania into the Ohio Valley.

A significant movement of Presbyterians to America came in the summer of 1718, to Boston from the Bann Valley around Coleraine, Ballymoney, Aghadowey and Macosquin. The Rev. William Boyd, of Macosquin, had been sent ahead to view out the land of their proposed adoption and his report of the lands and climate in the New England colony was highly favourable. The reasons given for emigration by these Presbyterians were not founded on materialism, but on matters of faith – to avoid oppression; to shun persecution; to cease from communications with idolators, and to secure freedom of worship.

The Rev. James MacGregor, minister of Aghadowey, was a guiding spirit in the whole operation. He was a sturdy individual, who at 11 years of age was a follower of Captain Adam Murray in defence of the city of Londonderry during the Siege of 1688-89. MacGregor lodged a petition for emigration of the Bann Valley Presbyterians with the Right Honourable Colonel Samuel Shute, Governor of the New England colony, and it was signed by ministerial colleagues, the Rev. Robert Higginbotham, of 1st Coleraine; the Rev. Henry Neille, of Ballyrashane; the Rev. James Thomson, of Ballywillan, the Rev.

Samuel Wilson and the Rev. Alexander McBride. In all 215 signatures were appended, and, of these, remarkably only seven were illiterate.

These Bann Valley Presbyterians had moved to Ulster from Argyllshire in Scotland in 1612 and for most of 100 years on Irish soil they had been continuously harried for their Covenanting faith. On the eve of departure the Rev. James MacGregor preached from the text: "If Thy presence go not with me, carry us not up hence".

They arrived at Boston on August 4, 1718 and, on the recommendation of James McKeen, of Ballymoney, the brother-in-law of MacGregor, settled initially at Casco Bay. They pushed their way up the Merrimac River, finally putting down their roots at Nutfield. James MacGregor led his flock like a shepherd and every enterprise was undertaken with reading, preaching and prayer. On the shores of Casco Bay they had sung together the 137th Psalm (By Babel's streams we sat and wept; when Zion we thought on; in midst thereof we hung our harps, the willow trees upon). And on arrival at Nutfield, MacGregor preached from Isaiah chapter 32, verse two – "And a man shall be as a hiding place from the wind and a covert from the tempest; as rivers of water in a dry place, as the shadow of a great rock in a weary land".

The Rev. James MacGregor lived until he was 97, six of his emigrant flock to 90. Those who settled the township of Nutfield were James McKeen, John Barnett, Archibald Clendenin, John Mitchell, James Starrett, James Anderson, Randal Alexander, James Gregg, James Clark, James Nesmith, Allen Anderson, Robert Weir, John Morrison, Samuel Allison, Thomas Steele and John Stuart.

Apart from the Nutfield settlement, the Bann Valley Presbyterians were involved in founding the townships of Pelham, Palmer, Windham, Chester, Merrimac, Goffstown, New Boston, Antrim, Peterborough, Acworth and Coleraine, in the states of New Hampshire, Vermont, Maine and Massachusetts. Nutfield, originally Indian land, was later changed to Londonderry, to comply with the requests of homesick families.

The MacGregor settlement lived mainly on potatoes, which they introduced from Ulster, bean porridge and barley broth. Tea and coffee were unknown in this part of America, but salmon and shad (herring-like fish) were plentiful in the rivers and lakes. Linen spinning became a popular industry, another legacy from life in Ulster.

5

Scots-Irish influences *in Charleston*

Charleston, main port of South Carolina, was the gateway to the Scots-Irish emigrants in the 18th century, a stepping stone to life in the Carolina piedmont area. This oldest and second largest city in South Carolina was settled by the British in 1670 and named after King Charles II. The first settlers were English, followed by French Huguenots, Scots-Irish, Germans and Swiss. The largest 18th century Jewish settlement in America was in Charleston and there has always been a large black population in the city, which has one of the finest collections of well-preserved colonial and antebellum homes and buildings in the United States.

The first Scottish Presbyterians to settle in South Carolina came in 1684 during the 'Killing Time' period in Scotland when Covenanters were killed for their faith. Some 146 Covenanters arrived at Charleston and settled at present-day Beaufort, establishing a colony known as Stuart's Town. This colony was attacked and destroyed by Spanish migrants.

When bounties were offered by the colonial government to prospective settlers in South Carolina from the 1730s, Charleston began to attract Scots-Irish immigrants in large numbers. By the 1760s the flow of people from Ulster to the Carolinas was so great that Charleston displaced New York as the second most important port of destination of emigrant vessels. Philadelphia was the main port and while New York's share of trade fell from 26 per cent to 15.7 in periods of heavy emigration, the share for Charleston rose from two per cent to 16.

Even after they passed through Charleston and settled 150-200 miles away in the Carolina up-country, the Scots-Irish community maintained links with the port in trade as farmers and merchants. Roads were extended from Charleston to settlements like the Waxhaws and Salisbury in Rowan County and trade was good.

Carrickfergus, Co. Antrim man Arthur Dobbs when he was Governor of North Carolina in the 1750s directed that a road be laid out from Salisbury to Charleston by way of Cold Water at the end of Lord Granville's line. Dobbs, in his diaries, stated: "Many on the lands had gone into indigo with good success, which they sell at Charleston having a wagon road to it, though 200 miles distant because our roads are not shortened and properly laid out. From the many merchants there, they afford them English goods cheaper, than at present in this province. The trade being in few hands they take a much higher price".

During the Revolutionary War, Charleston became one of the main theatres of the fighting, with British forces in control of the city from 1780 to 1782. President Andrew Jackson, then a young man, visited Charleston with his Co. Antrim born mother Elizabeth in September, 1780, and it was there that he developed his dislike for the British. His mother had moved to Charleston to nurse American soldiers imprisoned by the British there and before parting she is reported to have told Andrew: "Make friends by being honest; keep them by being steadfast, never tell a lie, nor take what is not your own, nor sue ... for slander ... settle them cases yourself".

Smitten by smallpox, Elizabeth Jackson died a few months later and she was buried in an unrecorded grave at Charles Town Neck, not far from the floating British prison ship. When told of his mother's death, Jackson's brief comment was: "I feel utterly alone". He later returned to Charleston in 1783 to receive a £400 legacy from his Irish grandfather Hugh Jackson, but before leaving the seaport he had squandered the money in gambling.

The Independent Presbyterian Church at Archdale Street in Charleston was largely the meeting house for Scots-Irish Presbyterian families in the years leading up to and during the Revolutionary War. One of the church's most colourful pastors was the Rev. William Tennent, from a distinguished Presbyterian family. Tennent's grandfather William was a close friend of the evangelist John

Whitefield and both he and his son William had emigrated from Ulster in the 1730s.

The Rev. William Tennent III, born at Freehold, New Jersey in 1740, was a graduate of Harvard and was licensed to preach by the New Brunswick Presbytery. He received a call to Independence Church in November, 1771 and delivered his first sermon the following April. The congregation grew and prospered under Tennent's ministry and his influence extended not just to clerical duties, but the great issue of the day – American independence.

He became a strong advocate of the patriot cause and was elected by the people of Charleston to the provincial congress of South Carolina. Tennent led his people from the front and, with several contemporaries, including Colonel Richard Richardson and the Hon. William Henry Drayton, he embarked on a tour of the Carolina up-country to "strengthen the friends of resistance and to win over the wavering". Public meetings were organised and sermons delivered in churches through the Piedmont, from Jackson's Creek at Fairfield and Rocky Creek, Chester, where the Co. Antrim Covenanting cleric the Rev. William Martin preached, to Boonesborough on the Long Cane Creek at Abbeville. On all occasions, after the religious services were over, Tennent addressed the people on the state of the country, gave them an up-date of events and collected money for the revolutionary cause.

Tennent even helped raise companies of militia when danger was imminent. He wrote prolifically in various publications in pursuit of independence and on January 11, 1777 delivered a speech in the House of Assembly in Charleston bitterly castigating the established status of the Church of England in the American colonies. His exhaustive efforts for ecclesiastical and civil freedom in the Charleston of his day and the Carolina Piedmont took its toll and shortly after his father died in March, 1777 William Tennent fell ill with a nervous fever at Sautee, 90 miles from Charleston, and within a few months he had passed away aged only 37.

William Tennent was described as "a very worthy and excellent minister of Christ, very Catholic, a fine scholar, a polite gentleman, a real exercised Christian". One of the last sermons he preached was from Philippians, chapter four, – "The Lord is at hand. Be careful for nothing, but in everything by prayer and supplication with thanksgiving let your requests be made known unto God." Tennent left five children, two sons and three daughters.

Descendants of this fiery frontier pastor and patriot still reside in the Charleston area and his memory lives on in South Carolina folklore. The monument to his memory in Independent Church reads: "He was distinguished for quickness of perception, solidity of judgment, energy and firmness of mind, for inflexible patriotism and ardent public spirit, for the boldness with which he enforced the claims of the Deity."

The United Kingdom

UNITED KINGDOM
Capital: London
Area: 244,017 sq km (94,215 sq miles)
Population: 57,800,000
Language: English
Religion: Christian
Currency: Pound sterling
Government: Monarchy

ENGLAND
Capital: London
Area: 130,360 sq km (50,332 sq miles)
Population: 48,071,300

NORTHERN IRELAND
Capital: Belfast
Area: 14,121 sq km (5,452 sq miles)
Population: 1,643,400

SCOTLAND
Capital: Edinburgh
Area: 78,769 sq km (30,412 sq miles)
Population: 5,148,600

WALES
Capital: Cardiff
Area: 20,767 sq km (8,018 sq miles)
Population: 2,936,800

Possession
nine-tenths of the law

Tomahawk rights was the description used for a form of squatting on lands by some Scots-Irish families in the early years of the American frontier settlements in the 18th century. The adage that possession was nine-tenths of the law was uppermost in the minds of Ulster emigrants who arrived on American shores with only the most meagre belongings they carried with them.

The colonial authorities in Pennsylvania and the Carolinas decreed nominal taxes as low as a penny an acre and the idea was to have the lands registered with the proper authorities. However, Ulster families who arrived at the ports of Philadelphia, New Castle (Delaware) and Charleston and were told to proceed west in a polite, orderly manner until they reached unoccupied territory had their own ideas.

Seeing vast stretches of unoccupied land as far as the eye could see they forcefully, with an independence of mind and purpose, declared: "It is against the law of God and nature, that so much land should be idle, while so many Christians wanted it to labour on, and to raise their bread". Even colonial agents sent by the Colonial governors to lands occupied illegally by the new wave of settlers were powerless to act, and with no police force as we know it the frontier people were virtually a law onto themselves.

No one was more exasperated by the practice of squatting, or tomahawk rights than Ulster-born William Logan, who was executive secretary to William Penn in Pennsylvania during the first two waves of immigration to America from the north of Ireland.

Logan, an aristocratic, bureaucratic Quaker from Lurgan in Co. Armagh, at first encouraged the movement to America of his native countrymen and in 1720 he said: "We were apprehensive from the Northern Indians. I therefore thought it might be prudent to plant a settlement of such men as those who formerly had so bravely defended Londonderry and Inniskillen (Enniskillen) as a frontier in case of any disturbance. These people if kindly used will be orderly as they have hitherto been and easily dealt with".

The urbane Logan rapidly become disenchanted with the Scots-Irish settlers he had done so much to encourage to emigrate and in 1724 he was calling them "bold and indigent strangers", who, when challenged for land titles, said they had been "solicited" for colonists in America and had come accordingly.

Later, Logan was to complain that "a settlement of five families from the north of Ireland gives me more trouble than fifty of any other people". He added: "They are troublesome settlers to the government and hard neighbours to the Indians".

But America was a harsh wilderness for human beings to exist and it was said that many of the rougher Scots-Irish traits which gentler European peoples regarded as weaknesses and vices turned out to be strengths and virtues on the frontier.

6

American Presidents *from the Carolinas*

The three American Presidents credited with being Tennesseans were born in the Carolinas and spent their childhood and youth there before heading into Tennessee to develop careers as lawyers, politicians and statesmen. Andrew Jackson was born at the Waxhaws, North Carolina in 1767; James Knox Polk close by in Mecklenburg County, North Carolina in 1795, and Andrew Johnson at Raleigh, North Carolina in 1808. All three were of Scots-Irish stock, with Jackson born only 18 months after his parents left Carrickfergus on the shores of Belfast Lough for a new life in America.

The Waxhaws region at the time was heavily populated by immigrant families from the North of Ireland who had arrived via Pennsylvania and the South Carolina port of Charleston and it was in this virtual wilderness that the Jacksons, with their relatives the Crawfords and the McKemeys and other kinsfolk from Ulster, set up home.

Andrew and Elizabeth Hutchinson Jackson, Andrew's parents, were linen weavers of lowland Scots roots who lived and worked in the first few years of their marriage at Boneybefore near Carrickfergus in East Co. Antrim. The couple left their homeland, with sons Hugh and Robert in 1765 and, after resting from their sea journey in Lancaster County, Pennsylvania, within a short time had acquired 200 acres of frontier farm land at Twelve Mile Creek in the Waxhaws. Times were hard on the American frontier and the Jacksons with others found the going tough. Young Andrew was born on March 15, 1767, a few weeks after his father's death, and Elizabeth Jackson was forced to take refuge with her sister Jane Crawford, who had also settled in the region with husband Robert and family. Branches of the Hutchinsons (Hutchison), Elizabeth Jackson's Co. Antrim family, had also settled in the Waxhaws region and at Long Cane (Abbeville in South Carolina). William Hutchinson was one of the earliest frontier settlers and the family married into the Mecklins or McLins, Scots-Irish immigrants from the same part of Ulster. They were involved in the establishment of the Presbyterian Church in the Long Cane (Abbeville) area of South Carolina.

Elizabeth Jackson was described as a woman "very conversive" and "industrious". It was said she spun flax beautifully, her heddie yarn spinning was the "best and finest ever seen". Andrew could read at five and at eight was able to write "a neat legible hand", and he could understand maps. Years later Andrew Jackson recalled long winter evenings when his mother told him and his brothers of the sufferings of their grandfather Hugh Jackson at the siege of Carrickfergus and the oppression by the nobility in Ireland of the labouring poor.

Andrew Jackson spent a turbulent youth in the rumbustious Carolina frontier country. It was the time of the Revolutionary struggle and, at 13, with his strongly independent streak and self-assuredness for one so young, he took part in the Battle of Hanging Rock and was involved in several skirmishes. Andrew's two brothers died in the Revolutionary War – Hugh from injuries received in battle and Robert from smallpox. Tragedy was to follow when his mother died from fever she had contracted when visiting relatives at a British prison ship at Charleston. Betty Jackson had been a strong-willed fearless individual who made a significant impact on the Carolina frontier and her son was to inherit these doughty characteristics.

The deaths left a big impression on Andrew, who was himself captured by British forces along with his brother Robert. Soldiers wrecked the house they were held captive in and an officer ordered Andrew to clean his boots. When he refused the officer struck him in the face with a sabre, cutting his upraised hand to the bone and leaving a scar on his head which he carried for life.

During the several years after the deaths of his mother and brothers, Andrew Jackson had many violent run-ins with the authorities. He was hot-tempered, and with a reckless streak, and engaged in tavern and street brawls. He managed to squander a £400 inheritance from his grandfather Hugh Jackson back in Ireland and 200 acres of his father's farmland through gambling.

Andrew was trained as a saddler and for a time the company he kept while living as a teenager at Salisbury, North Carolina was not good. Notoriously his reputation went ahead of him even as far as Charleston in South Carolina. However, he was a teacher at the age of 17 and studied law. In 1787, at the age of 20, he was admitted to the North Carolina bar, practising at Anson County in the town of Monroe. He soon became public prosecutor of North Carolina's western district and from this posting turned his attention towards Tennessee, and Nashville where his career was to take a very definite upward swing over the next few years. Jackson, it was said, sowed his wild oats in Salisbury, Rowan County. While in the White House he was reminded by an associate that he was once from Salisbury, North Carolina to which the President replied: "Old Salisbury, yes, I remember well. I was quite a lad there." Rowan County tradition says Jackson, then only about 17, was "the most roaring, rollicking, game-cocking, card-playing, mischievous fellow that ever lived in Salisbury." On the frontier at the time this was the practice of a good few settlers, but Jackson later said that he was but a raw lad then, "but I did my best."

In 1791 Jackson married Rachel Donelson, daughter of Colonel John Donelson, a Scots-Irish frontiersman of note who founded the city of Nashville in 1780. From this region Jackson directed his talents as a lawyer, soldier, politicians and statesman which were to culminate in his two terms as American President in 1829-1837.

In the journal of C.W. Clerk, itinerant minister in South Carolina, 1766-68, the Waxhaws settlement was reported as having a Presbyterian meeting house and a pastor, Scotsman the Rev. William Richardson, described as being "a good sort of man". The congregation was very large with seldom less than 1,000 assembled for Sunday service.

James Knox Polk, the 11th President of the United States, had ancestral links to Paisley, Renfrewshire in Scotland, and East Donegal and Londonderry in the north of Ireland. The Polks were a well established Presbyterian family who had owned extensive lands in Ireland and had fought in the various wars there, on the side of the Protestant Williamite cause of the late 17th century.

The Polks arrived in Pennsylvania and the first settler, Robert Polk (Pollock), was an elder in the Old Rehobeth Presbyterian Church, claimed to be the oldest Presbyterian meeting house in America. Many of the connection settled in North Carolina and prospered, largely through the surveying work of Ezekiel Polk and his son Samuel, James Knox Polk's father.

The Polks had lived at Mecklenburg County, where James Knox was born, since the earliest Scots-Irish settlement in the region of the 1740s. One of the clan, Thomas, said to be a man of "great athleticness, of much energy of both body and mind", had led the way from Pennsylvania trekking down the Great Wagon Road through the valley of Virginia. He crossed the Yadkin Rover in up-country North Carolina and came upon a fertile region, watered by a network of creeks flowing south and west into the Catawbe River. There he cleared land, built one of the first cabins on Sugar Creek, and married a daughter of the first white settler west of the Yadkin. Thomas was soon followed by the rest of the family, including the Alexanders, other Ulster-Scots immigrants who married Polks.

Mecklenburg County in North Carolina has had per capita the most dominant strain of Scots-Irish settlements of any region in the United States, except for Pittsburgh, Pennsylvania and Augusta and Rockbridge Counties in Virginia. Mecklenburg was also where a document was drawn up by the citizens, mainly Scots-Irish, on May 20, 1775 which pledged to break the ties with English rule. This was to be the forerunner of the July 4, 1776 Declaration of Independence and a Mecklenburg resident who signed was Thomas Polk. He was a general and colonel in the North Carolina militia, serving at both the battles of Brandywine and Germantown. His son William was also a colonel in the revolutionary militia.

James Knox Polk was a graduate of the University of North Carolina, finishing in 1815 at the head of his class. Earlier, most of his childhood had been spent in Mecklenburg County, heavily influenced by his staunchly Presbyterian mother, Jane Knox. His grandfather

Ezekiel and father Samuel spent long periods away from home on their surveying work. Jane Knox was the daughter of James Knox from Iredell County, North Carolina, a captain in the Revolutionary Army.

In 1806, much against the wishes of Jane Knox Polk, the family decided to lift their roots and head for new fertile lands in Middle Tennessee surveyed by Ezekiel and Robert. The 500-mile journey into barren territory took six weeks to complete by covered wagon and Robert and his young family set up home at Duck River, a settlement close to the present day town of Columbia in Maury County. This had been a wilderness region before 1800 – a place where no white person would have inhabited except surveyors and hunters. It was Indian hunting ground, although the native tribes did not live there.

James Knox Polk grew to manhood in Maury County as his family prospered in business and land transaction in Columbia. It was there, as a lawyer, that he made preparation for a distinguished political career as a Democrat which included seven terms in Congress, Speaker of the House, and President from 1845 to 1849. He was a President with family roots in Ulster, blooded in North Carolina and accepted as a naturalised Tennessean

Andrew Johnson, the third American President associated with Tennessee, lived the first 18 years of his life in the Carolinas. He was born in Raleigh, North Carolina on December 29, 1808 and his father Jacob, said to have occupied humble positions of trust in the community, died when Andrew was quite young. The Johnsons were a third generation Scots-Irish family, Andrew's grandfather of the same name emigrated from Larne in Co. Antrim in 1750. They settled in a Carolina community which was known as "the poor Protestants".

Andrew was apprenticed at the age of 10 to J.J. Shelby, a tailor of Raleigh, and with literally no prior education in life his only means of learning was through meeting and talking with people. One gentleman of Raleigh who regularly visited the tailor's shop read to the workmen from The American Speaker periodical, containing selections from the great orators and writers of America and England. The speeches of William Pitt and Edmund Burke excited young Johnson.

In 1824, just before the end of his apprenticeship, Andrew left Raleigh and secured journey work at Laurens Courthouse in South Carolina. He remained there for 20 months, but returned to Raleigh and offered J.J. Shelby the 10 dollar reparation caused by leaving his apprenticeship. Shelby required some bond of indemnity against loss which Andrew could not give and Johnson decided it was time to move west to Tennessee. On the journey across the Appalachian Mountains in September 1826, Andrew was joined by his mother Mrs. Mary McDonough Dougherty, her second husband Turner Dougherty and his older brother. It was said they travelled the road by which Andrew Jackson had entered Tennessee 40 years earlier, their sparse belongings packed on a little one-horse wagon.

Greeneville, was a strong Scots-Irish village settlement nestled in the foothills of the Great Smoky Mountains and as Andrew and his family were of this kith they were warmly welcomed. The postmaster in Greeneville was William Dixon (Dickson), a Covenanter of Ulster stock, and with John A. Brown, a clerk at the Dixon store, they persuaded Andrew to stay and pursue his tailor's trade. There he met his wife Eliza McArdle, the only daughter of a Scots-Irish shoemaker, and it was her ambition and drive which helped push Andrew up the social scale. Johnson ran his tailor's shop, but he increasingly interested himself in the affairs of the region, took part in debates in the village square, or at Greeneville College and Tusculum Academy, which was founded by Scots-Irish pioneering pastor, the Rev. Samuel Doak. He became an alderman and eventually rose to be Mayor of Greeneville, and Governor of Tennessee for two terms.

He became a senator in 1857 and in the White House was much involved with Abraham Lincoln in the moves to abolish slavery. His Union tendencies were disliked in the South, he was labelled "a home-made Yankee", but still maintained a solid support base in the Greeneville area of East Tennessee. During the Civil War, Andrew left the Senate at Abraham Lincoln's request to become military governor of Tennessee and it was while serving in that post that he was nominated Vice-President in 1865. On President Lincoln's assassination on April 14, 1865, Johnson was elevated to the Presidency and he served almost four years until 1869.

President Woodrow Wilson, whose grandfather James Wilson emigrated from Strabane in Co. Tyrone in 1807, lived for a time in Columbia, South Carolina when his father was professor of pastoral theology at the local seminary. Woodrow, born at Staunton in the

Shenandoah Valley of Virginia in 1856, was 14 at the time of the movement to Columbia, where his mother's people the Woodrows had lived. It was a highly formative period in Woodrow Wilson's life, the years just before he entered the College of New Jersey, now Princeton.

The Wilsons worshipped in First Columbia Presbyterian Church and his parents Joseph Ruggles and Jessie Woodrow Wilson are buried in the cemetery there. Dr. Wilson had been earlier minister of First Staunton Presbyterian Church and the Presbyterian Church in Augusta, Georgia. The Wilsons lived at 1705 Hampton Street, Columbia, which today is preserved as the Woodrow Wilson Museum by the South Carolina Historical Commission and the American Legion of South Carolina. The two-storey white frame house was designed by his mother, who personally supervised its construction, and among family mementoes is the bed in which the President was born. In the garden are four magnolia trees and a sweet olive tree planted by Mrs. Wilson.

Woodrow Wilson was intensely proud of his Ulster-Scots roots, and in 1919, the year after he was elected to his first term as Democratic President, he said: "I am sorry to say that my information about my father's family is very meagre. My father's father was born in the North of Ireland, he had no brothers on this side of the water. The family came from the neighbourhood I have understood as Londonderry."

James Wilson, an apprentice printer was 20 when he left his home at Dergelt, two miles from Strabane and 12 miles from Londonderry and his wife Anne Adams was also Ulster-born. They married in Fourth Philadelphia Presbyterian Church in 1808 and had 10 children, seven sons and three daughters. The youngest and seventh son of seven sons was Joseph Ruggles Wilson, Woodrow's father.

Woodrow Wilson once described his nature as a struggle between his Irish blood – "quick, generous, impulsive, passionate, anxious always to help and to sympathise with those in distress" and his Scotch blood – "canny, tenacious and perhaps a little exclusive". On receiving an honorary degree at Harvard in the spring of 1907 Wilson said: "The beauty about a Scotch-Irishman is that he not only thinks he is right, but knows he is right". And he added: "I have not departed from the faith of my ancestors."

People *of principle*

"The Scotch-Irish Presbyterians who settled the hill country of South Carolina were a sturdy breed. These men came with rifle in one hand and Psalm book in the other. They cleared the forest and used some of the first logs they cut in building forts for the protection of their wives and little ones against the Indians; and in erecting churches in which, with their families, they might worship the God of the Covenant. In some instances they raised a church while their families were still camping out. Their ministers preached the doctrine that 'resistance to tyrants is obedience to God.' These people believed and were the bone and sinew of the Whig cause in the days of the Revolution. These Scotch-Irish Presbyterians would argue all day about a spoonful of hominy if there was a little principle in the bottom of the spoon. That they could use the axe and the plow as well as their tongues, our corn crowned and cotton clothed hills today testify. That they were as ready with hunting-shirt, powder-horn and rifle as with the weapons of argument, our land is a witness."

- **William S. Morrison**
Professor of History and Political Economy
Clemson College, Fort Hill, South Carolina
September 1890

7

The Scots-Irish roots
of President Jimmy Carter

President Jimmy Carter is Scots-Irish on his father's side and can trace his roots back to Andrew Cowan, one of the earliest settlers of Boonesborough near Abbeville in South Carolina. Andrew Cowan (1742-86) was one of the group of mainly Ulster emigrant families who were settled in a buffer territory between white and Cherokee Indian lands at Long Cane in the Carolina up-country between 1763 and 1775.

Sophronia Caroline Cowan Pratt, the great grand-daughter of Andrew Cowan, was great-grandmother of President Carter, who was born at Plains, Georgia in 1924 not so far away from the South Carolina homeland of his descendants. A daughter of James E. and Sophronia Caroline Pratt, Nina Pratt married William Archibald Carter from Georgia and his son James Earl Carter was the President's father.

It has not been established what part of Ulster Andrew Cowan came from or his port of entry to America. The Cowans very probably were a Co. Antrim family – the surname is common today in Northern Ireland, where until now Jimmy Carter had not been acknowledged as one of the Scots-Irish Presidents. Some of the first Boonesborough families came into Charleston, others into Philadelphia and after a spell in Pennsylvania moved to South Carolina via the Shenandoah Valley of Virginia. Andrew Cowan was allocated 300 acres of land at Boonesborough on February 23, 1772 and his wife Ann (1745-1831) and he had seven children, three sons and four daughters, who married into other Scots-Irish families of the region – the

Brownlees, Seawrights, Hawthornes and Richeys. It was from Isaac Cowan, Andrew's eldest son, and his son John that the Carter link was eventually forged. Isaac (1764-1831) married Jane Seawright (1771-1859), who was also of Scots-Irish extraction, and their son John (1805-74) married Sarah B. Clinkscales (1811-52).

John Cowan was a prosperous resident of Due West township, which emerged from Boonesborough settlement and today his home, known as the Pink House, is the oldest property still standing in the locality. Like the other Boonesborough families, the Cowans were Presbyterians.

President Carter was elected to the White House as a Democrat in November, 1976, narrowly defeated Republican Gerry Ford. He was the first Deep South President since Zachary Taylor in 1848 and served one term. A strong Baptist, Jimmy Carter sustained intense pressure as President during the American hostages in Iran crisis of 1979-81 and it is arguable that this cost him a second term in the White House. In his retirement years, Jimmy Carter has devoted much time to humanitarian work, both in the United States and abroad. Carter had many detractors, but he earned this tribute from former House of Representatives speaker, Irish American Thomas P. "Tip" O'Neill – "When it came to understanding the issues of the day, Jimmy Carter was the smartest public official I've ever known. The range and extent of his knowledge were astounding, he could speak with authority about energy, the nuclear issue, space travel, the Middle East, Latin America, human rights, American history and just about any other topic that came up".

Members of the Cowan clan, George and John, were recorded as settling at Rowan County in North Carolina in 1750, in what was known as the Irish settlement west of the Yadkin River. The Cowans were in Pennsylvania as early as 1721 and had moved to North Carolina via the Great Wagon Road. One of this family, Captain Thomas Cowan, engaged on the patriot side at the battles of Kings Mountain, Cowpens, Ramsour's Mile and Cowan's Ford.

THE SCOTS-IRISH PRESIDENTS

Thirteen of the 41 Presidents of the United States can now be traced back to Scots-Irish ancestry: three (Andrew Jackson, James Buchanan and Chester Alan Arthur) came from first generation parents.

- **Andrew Jackson:** (Democrat – 7th President 1829-37). Born on March 15, 1767 in the Waxhaw region of North Carolina, his family had left Ulster in 1765, having lived in the village of Boneybefore near Carrickfergus. Andrew helped draft the constitution for Tennessee, which became the 16th State of the Union on June 1, 1796.

- **James K. Polk:** (Democrat – 11th President 1845-49). Born on November 2, 1795 near Charlotte in North Carolina, he is descended from a Robert Polk (Pollok) of Londonderry, who had arrived in the American colonies about 1680. Was a Governor of Tennessee and he and his wife Sarah are buried in the State Capital in Nashville.

- **James Buchanan:** (Democrat – 15th President 1857-61). Born on April 23, 1791 in Mercersburg, Pennsylvania, he was born into a Presbyterian home like his predecessors Jackson and Polk. The family came originally from Deroran near Omagh, Co. Tyrone and left Donegal for America in 1783.

- **Andrew Johnson:** (Democrat – 17th President 1865-69). Born on December 29, 1808 in Raleigh, North Carolina, his namesake and grandfather from Mounthill outside Larne had come to America about 1750, from Larne, Co. Antrim. He rose to the Presidency from humble log cabin origins and worked as a tailor for many years.

- **Ulysses Simpson Grant:** (Republican – 18th President 1869-77). The man who commanded the Union Army in the American Civil War, his mother Hannah Simpson was descended from the Simpson family of Dergenagh near Dungannon, Co. Tyrone. His great grandfather John Simpson had left Ulster for America in 1760.

- **Chester Alan Arthur:** (Republican – 21st President 1881-85). Born on October 5, 1830 in Fairfield, Vermont, his grandfather and father, Baptist pastor William Arthur, emigrated to the United States from Dreen near Cullybackey in Co. Antrim in 1801.

- **Grover Cleveland:** (Democrat – 22nd and 24th President 1885-89 and 1893-97). Born on March 8, 1837 in Caldwell, New Jersey, his maternal grandfather Abner Neal had left Co. Antrim in the late 18th century. Son of a Presbyterian minister.

- **Benjamin Harrison:** (Republican – 23rd President 1889-93). Born on August 20, 1833 at North Bend, Ohio, two of his great grandfathers James Irwin and William McDowell were Ulstermen.

- **William McKinley:** (Republican – 25th President 1897-1901). Born on January 29, 1843 in Niles, Ohio, he was the great grandson of James McKinley, who had emigrated to America from Conagher, near Ballymoney in Co. Antrim about 1743.
- **Woodrow Wilson:** (Democrat – 28th President 1913-21). Born December 28, 1856 in Staunton, Virginia, he was the grandson of James Wilson, who had emigrated to North Carolina from Dergalt, Co. Tyrone about 1807. His father Dr. Joseph Ruggles Wilson was a Presbyterian minister.
- **Richard Millhouse Nixon:** (Republican – 37th President 1969-74). Born on January 13, 1913 in Yorba Linda, California, he had Ulster connections on two sides of his family. His Nixon ancestor left Co. Antrim for America around 1753, while the Millhouses came from Carrickfergus and Ballymoney. He died in 1994.
- **James Earl Carter:** (Democrat – 39th President 1976-81). Born on October 1, 1924 in Plains, Georgia. Scots-Irish settler Andrew Cowan, the great grandfather of President Jimmy Carter's great grandmother on his father's side, was one of the first residents of Boonesborough, South Carolina in 1772. Andrew Cowan was a Presbyterian, President Carter is a Baptist.
- **William Jefferson Clinton:** (Democrat – 41st President 1993-). Born on August 19, 1946 in Hope, Hempstead County, Arkansas. President Bill Clinton claims to be five times removed from Lucas Cassidy, who left Co. Fermanagh for America around 1750. Lucas Cassidy was of Presbyterian stock, President Clinton is a Baptist.

Letter from President Jimmy Carter
453, Freedom. Parkway
Atlanta, Georgia.

May 17, 1997

To Billy Kennedy,
   The only information I have about Andrew Cowan is that he was born about 1742, died 1786 in Abbeville County, South Carolina, married Ann, who was born about 1745, and died in 1831 in the same county. Isaac Cowan was born in 1764, died December 25, 1831, married Jane Seawright (1771-1859) and their son (1805-1874) married Sarah B Clinkscales (1811-1852). I guess you have more than this, which I would appreciate knowing. Best wishes.

Thanks, Jimmy Carter.

8

Maghera's Charles Thomson -
"the venerable patriot"

Few people put their personal stamp on the history of the United States quite like Charles Thomson, the man who designed the Great American Seal and notified George Washington of his election as the nation's first President. Thomson was arguably the most influential statesman in the early formative years of America.

This Ulster-born Presbyterian was the secretary of the American Continental Congress for 15 years from 1774 and when the new federal constitution was adopted in 1789 Thomson was delegated to convey to Washington at his Mount Vernon, Virginia home the request that he become first head of state. He brought Washington to New York to be inaugurated and then formally resigned his own position, handing over to the new President all the records of Congress and the Great Seal. Thomson, then 60, quietly retired from the scene.

The original Declaration of Independence of July 4, 1776 bore only two signatures, that of John Hancock, the President of Congress, and Charles Thomson. There was no great rush of members to sign, for if independence had not been achieved and sustained those whose names were on the document would undoubtedly have been tried by the British and almost certainly executed.

On the first printed copy of the Declaration the only other name visible was that of printer John Dunlap, like Thomson, Ulster-born, from Strabane. The later engrossed Declaration, written on parchment, was not ready until August. It was signed by every member of Congress, but, for reasons best known to himself, Thomson did not sign it. In effect, the later document hailed as "The Declaration" was not actually a legal document as it was not signed by the secretary.

The remarkable story of how this eminent high-ranking American statesman reached such a pinnacle of power is surely part of the great American dream where opportunity arose for folk from as humble a background as Charles Thomson experienced in his north of Ireland homeland.

Charles Thomson was born in the townland of Gorteade, Upperlands near the town of Maghera, Co. Londonderry in November, 1729. His father John combined linen weaving with farming in the desolate foothills of the Sperrin mountain range and he and his wife Mary had six children; five sons and one daughter – William, Alexander, Charles, Matthew, John and Mary. It was at the birth of the last child that Mary Houston Thomson tragically died and John Thomson had the onerous task of single-handedly rearing his family.

With the death of his wife John Thomson's thoughts turned to a new life in the American colonies as word reached back to Ulster that land was plentiful there and opportunity abounded. There had been a succession of bad harvests in Ulster up to 1729 and money was scarce. Rents were high, the annual rent per acre of land was £20 and for this sum an acre could be purchased in America.

The Thomson family, who were linked to a lowland Scottish clan from a century before, belonged to Maghera Presbyterian Church and John and Mary's children were all baptised there. In 1739, John and his young care headed for America, sailing from Londonderry to Philadelphia. It was a rough passage for the Thomson family and tragedy struck when the ship entered Delaware Bay, John Thomson, worn out looking after his young family, took ill and died to the anguish of his children.

Years later, Charles Thomson recalled: "I stood by the bedside of my expiring and much loved father, closed his eyes and performed the last filial duties to him." The body was buried at sea to save the cost of a land burial and the ship's captain unscrupulously held on to John Thomson's monies deposited in the ship's safe at the beginning of the journey.

Had John Thomson lived his American interests would have been directed into agriculture and it is believed one of the sons moved into farming. Charles chose a different course in life after a quite inauspicious start. He was placed in the care of a blacksmith in Pennsylvania and treated very well. One night, however, he overhead the blacksmith and his wife talking about having him indentured as an apprentice and, uneasy about his future, he ran away. Folklore has it he met by chance on his travels a kindly and wealthy lady, who, on learning of his circumstances, arranged that he be placed in the new classical school at Thunder Hill, New London, Pennsylvania. There, Thomson was taught by Ulster-born Presbyterian minister the Rev. Dr. Francis Allison, originally from Leck outside Letterkenny in Co. Donegal.

Thomson graduated as a teacher in 1750 and taught Greek and Latin at Philadelphia Academy, the forerunner of the University of Philadelphia. But in 1760, at the age of 31, he gave up teaching to enter business and soon built up a reputation as a successful merchant. Earlier in 1757, he had been selected by the Delaware Indians as their secretary at the negotiations leading to the Treaty of Easton.

The Indian chief Teedyuscung, who called himself King, was particularly annoyed at the "Walking Purchase Treaties". These ensured lands purchased from the Indians were measured by how far a man could walk in a day and a relay of runners was employed by the white settlers to maximise the area covered. Thomson's fairness and integrity won some concessions for the Delaware Indians, who gave him the name "Wegh-Wu-Haw-Mo-Land" – the man who speaks the truth.

Thomson's first wife died in childbirth, and, in 1774, he remarried Hannah Harrison, from a wealthy Pennsylvanian family. It was in that year that Thomson became involved with the first Continental Congress meeting in Philadelphia, as secretary.

Politically, Charles Thomson was originally involved with the Whig movement, but his dislike of the English was deeply engrained and he enthusiastically espoused the Revolutionary cause once installed in the Continental Congress. When Independence was declared in 1776, Benjamin Franklin, Thomas Jefferson and John Adams were appointed to design a seal for the new state. Six years on, their work had not been fulfilled and Charles Thomson was tasked with the design, and within a week he had a mould ready for Congress. He was helped by William Barton, a young Pennsylvanian lawyer and the seal was written into law on June 20, 1782. From Thomson's imaginative design emerged the Great Seal which today is the distinctive public sign of the American nation and its Presidential administration. The Great Seal has never been changed, although artistic variations have been made as new dies were prepared. In all seven dies were cut – in 1782, 1825, 1841, 1854, 1877, 1885 and 1904.

In retirement, Charles Thomson spent most of his time translating the Old and New Testaments of the Bible from the Greek Septuagint version. This outstanding work was not instantly acclaimed for its worth and it was said that after his death copies were sold as wastepaper.

Charles Thomson died on August 16, 1824, aged 95. He was buried, as per his wish, alongside wife Hannah in the family plot at Harriton, Pennsylvania. However, when a new cemetery was developed some years later at Laurel Hill, four miles north of Philadelphia, a nephew John Thomson was persuaded to apply for the removal of his uncle's remains. It is thought the burial of the Thomsons would give the cemetery status. Other family members objected, but with friends a ghoulish John Thomson proceeded in 1838 to illegally remove the remains of Charles and Hannah Thomson to take them for re-burial at Laurel Hill. A 16-foot high obelisk weighing five tonnes was placed over the grave.

Down the years, Charles Thomson has been referred to by historians as the first Prime Minister of the United States. He virtually ran the American government in the transition period from the end of the Revolutionary War until George Washington's election as President. He was the "venerable patriot", from a humble background at Maghera, Co. Londonderry.

Leaders of *church and state*

66 The Scotch-Irish people with their intense
Presbyterianism not only built up a great church in
America where they had been transplanted, but
when time came they were a leading and most powerful
factor in building up a great state, leaving their impression
distinctly engraved on its organic law. At the outbreak of
the American Revolution, these Scotch-Irish Presbyterians
were scattered from New Hampshire to Georgia and they
espoused the revolutionary cause with much intensity.
When the Declaration of Independence in 1776 turned the
13 colonies into 13 American states, seven of the first governors were of this people. In Virginia, they raised the
question of the complete separation of church and state,
and they pressed the matter continuously with energy and
vigour until the cause was won. The effect of this great
victory was soon felt in all the states, and when the federal constitution was presented for adoption, it was mainly
their combined and powerful influence which secured that
most important amendment, that 'Congress shall make no
law respecting an establishment of religion, or prohibiting
the free exercise thereof'. The honour and glory of these
wonderful achievements for the church and for the state,
unquestionably belong to the Scotch-Irish people. There

was not a body of people in the American colonies who understood and appreciated these important measures, as they did. The severe discipline and persecution in their Ireland homes had caused these great principles to take deep root in their minds and heart.   **99**

– an address delivered by the **Rev. J. H. Bryson** at the centennial of First Presbyterian Church, Columbia, South Carolina, November 7, 1894.

Authority on Indian culture

Co. Antrim-born James Adair was an Indian trader and author of note in South Carolina during the latter part of the 18th century.

Adair, born in 1709, emigrated to America in 1735 and, from his tavern at Cherokee Ford, developed trade with the Indians of South Carolina. He was recognised by the tribes as a diplomat and peace envoy and in his book "History of the American Indians" he theorised that the Indians were descended from the lost tribes of Israel. His detailed observations at close hand with the native Americans made the book valuable to ethnologists and students of 18th century literature. Adair died in North Carolina in 1783.

Indian tribes in South and North Carolina included the Cherokees, Siouans, Catawabas, Creeks, Shawnees, Choctaws and Chickasaws.

9

First Carolina townships
founded by Scots-Irish

The small South Carolina town of Donalds, formerly Donaldsville, is named after Samuel Donnald, whose Ballynure, Co. Antrim-born father John settled in the area in 1800. John Donnald, who was 20 when he arrived in America, became an elder of Greenville Presbyterian Church in the town and his wife Mary Houston was from the same part of Ulster, a kin of General Sam Houston. Samuel Donnald, the postmaster of Donalds, was also an elder in Greenville Church and a leading community leader. Donalds township was set up in 1842.

Donalds is derived from the township of Boonesborough, named after the English Quaker frontiersman Daniel Boone, and settled by Scots-Irish immigrants between 1763 and 1775. This was a settlement for families who had entered the port of Charleston from Ulster and when surveyed first in 1762 by Patrick Calhoun, father of eminent South Carolina statesman John C. Calhoun, it consisted of 20,500 acres. The early settlement served as a buffer zone between the Cherokee Indian tribes and immigrants in the South Carolina low country and to qualify to settle in Boonesborough township one had to be a Protestant in good standing. This was not a problem for the Presbyterian families from Co. Antrim who brought their Bibles and catechisms in the long journey across the Atlantic.

The Cherokees had lived in the region for several centuries, hunting and trading and some of the native American place names still exist to this day. Boonesborough never developed as a proper town and it was left to Donalds and Due West to progress as identifiable communities.

Most of the first Boonesborough settlers came from East Co. Antrim, from Larne and neighbouring hamlets of Raloo, Islandmagee, Glynn, Kilwaughter and Ballynure. Families listed in the 1762-75 settlements were: Agnew, Barr, Baxter, Bayley, Beatty, Bingham, Brown, Brownlee, Campbell, Corkery, Colvill, Cowan, Dixon, Dickson, Duffield, Fee, Ferguson, Fisher, Forsith, Frazier, Gaillard, Gray, Gregg, Hannah, Hathorn, Herron, Hetherington, Hunter, Johnson, Kingan, Lesslie, McCracklin, McCullock, Miller, Montgomery, Moor, Moore, Paxton, Perry, Purse, Ross, Seawright, Smith, Templeton, Thompson, Walker, Wallace and Webb.

Many of the early settlers were involved in the revolutionary struggle during the War of Independence and their descendants sided with the Confederacy in the Civil War. John Donnald served in the Revolutionary War as a patriot, rising to major and his wife was a grand-daughter of Captain Robert Armstrong, of the Colonial militia.

Donalds, today with a population of less than 1,000, is noted as a township of serenity, which extends along its one main street where little groups of farmers collect regularly under the shade of tall oaks. Three miles from Donalds is the slightly larger township of Due West, where it was once said that the Sabbath was so cherished by the God-fearing residents there, that roosters crowing on Sunday were apt to find themselves in a stew on Monday. Even the railway in Due West had for generations a Sunday ban.

Near here an important treaty was completed on May 20, 1777, when Cherokee tribes signed away extensive land claims in South Carolina. This followed an invasion of the region by militiamen led by Governor Andrew Pickens, the son of Ulster immigrants.

An historical marker for Boonesborough at Donalds reads: "Surveyed in 1762 by Patrick Calhoun and named for Government by Thomas Boone, this 20,500-acre township was one of four townships laid out west of Ninety Six as a buffer between white and Cherokee lands. In 1763 Scots-Irish families began to settle in the area near Long Cane, Park's and Chickasaw Creeks. The headquarters of Long Cane Creek are 500 feet south; the Cherokee path crossed the township boundary one mile south".

10

Covenanting stock who
peopled the Carolinas

The Rev. William Martin, a highly colourful pastor of the Covenanting tradition, was synonymous with the Scots-Irish Presbyterian settlements in the South Carolina up-country during the late 18th century. As the first Covenanting minister in the region, Ulster-born Martin was not only a uncompromising advocate of the gospel, but fearless in his opposition to the High Church-influenced British authorities who had discriminated against his people in the north of Ireland and on the American frontier.

William Martin belonged to the Reformed Presbyterian Church in Ireland and, it was after a period of excessive rent demands and evictions of tenants and their homesteads, that he declared from his pulpit in Ballymoney, Co. Antrim that "enough was enough".

"Anyone who knows anything about the Ulster countryside realises that the rents are so high that the land does not bring in enough to pay them. Many of us are beggared and in time all would be", he told his congregation in 1772, stating that as a minister he could not stand idly by and await the violence and ruin that would come. "Steps should be taken now to see that such situations did not develop", was Martin's advice. He proposed that they all pool their limited resources and send to Belfast to charter ships for emigration to South Carolina where they would "obtain free land and live free men".

William Martin, the son of David Martin, was born at Ballyspollum (Ballyspallan) near Ballykelly, Co. Londonderry in 1729. He was ordained as a minister of the Reformed Presbyterian Church at The

Vow near Rasharkin in Co. Antrim in 1757 and was appointed to the charge of the nearby Ballymoney congregation. His education in theology had been obtained at the University of Glasgow and he became active in establishing Reformed (Covenanting) Churches across the north of Ireland. By 1763 there were sufficient ministers to form a Reformed Presbytery of Ireland.

The Ballymoney congregation agreed they must leave their homeland if life was to be made humanly bearable, and with other Covenanters they left for Charleston in South Carolina in five ships. In all 467 families (more than 1,000 people) huddled together on the arduous nine-week journey across the Atlantic in the autumn of 1772, in five wooden vessels: James and Mary, Lord Dunluce, Pennsylvania Farmer, Hopewell and Free Mason.

The sailings of 1772 were recorded by the Belfast News Letter thus:

James and Mary – 200 tons. Master – John Workman; agents – James McVicker and John Moore. On July 29, hoped that passengers would be punctual and allow vessel to sail August 8. Sailed from Larne on August 25, 1772.

Lord Dunluce – 400 tons. Master – James Gillis; agents – John Montgomery; Rev. William Martin (Kellswater) and William Barklie (Ballymena). On Saturday August 28 advertised that passengers should give earnest before September 5 as more offered to go than can be taken; but on September 15 announced some families drawn back so can accommodate 200 passengers more. The ship finally sailed from Larne, October 4, 1772.

Pennsylvania Farmer – 350 tons. Master – Charles Robinson; agents – John Ewing, S. Brown and Rev. John Logue (Broughshane). Sailing postponed to allow farmers to dispose of their crops; sailed from Belfast, October 16, 1772.

Hopewell – 250 tons. June 16 advertised arrival in England from South Carolina; a minister urgently needed advertised. Master – J. Ash; agents – William Beatty; sailed from Belfast with Captain Martin, Master, on October 19, 1772.

Free Mason – 250 tons. Master – John Semple; agents – W. and G. Glenry, Hill Wilson, George Anderson, William Booth. Sailed from Newry, October 27, 1772.

It was later recorded that the James and Mary arrived at Charleston on October 18 with 200 settlers on board. Some other vessels with a greater number on board were soon to follow this. Because some passengers had smallpox the ships were not permitted to clear for embarkation for several weeks. Strict quarantine was observed on the ships if disease was confirmed.

It was a custom for passengers of emigrant ships to express their appreciation for treatment aboard ship and to write a letter for publication. Even in the midst of illness this was not forgotten and a letter from passengers of the James and Mary appeared in the Belfast News Letter on December 22, 1772:

"To Mr. James M'Vickar, Merchant in Larne.

Charles-Town, Oct. 21, 1772

Sir,
These will inform you, that we arrived here all well and in good spirits the 18th instant (five children excepted who died in the passage) after a pleasant and agreeable passage of seven weeks and one day. – Pleasant with respect to weather, and agreeable with regard to the concord and harmony that subsisted among us all: and, to confirm what we have heard you assert, before we left Ireland, we must say, that we had more than a sufficiency of all kinds of provisions, and good in their kind: and to speak of Captain Workman, as he justly deserves, we must say with the greatest truth (and likewise with the greatest thanks and gratitude to him) that he treated us all with the greatest tenderness and humanity: and seemed even desirous of obliging any one, whom it might be in his power to serve. If you think proper, we would be desirous you should cause these things to be inserted in the public News Letter, being sensible they will afford our friends and acquaintances great satisfaction; and we hope they may be of some use to you and Captain

Workman, if you resolve to trade any more in the passenger way. Now, in confirmation of these things, we subscribe ourselves as follows:

We are, Sir, you most humble servants, Revd. Robert McClintock, John Peddan, Joseph Lowry, Timothy McClintock, Nathan Brown, Samuel Kerr, James Peddan, Alex. Brown, John Brown, Thomas Madill, Wm. Simpson, John McClintock, John Dicky, James Hood, John Montgomery, John Snody, John Caldwell, Robt. Hadden, Wm. Boyd, Robt. Machesney, Wm. Eashler, Charles Miller, John Rickey, Charles Dunlop, Thos. Makee, James Stinson, Wm. Anderson, John Thompson, Hugh Loggan, Peter Willey, David Thompson, Hugh Mansoad, Robt, Wilson, Robt, Ross, John Parker, James Young, Robt. Neile.

P.S. We had sermons every Sabbath, which was great satisfaction to us. We omitted to let you know, that the Mate, Mr. Boal, as also the common hands, behaved with great care and benevolence towards us."

The passengers on the *Lord Dunluce* also wrote a letter of commendation for the ship and Captain, which appeared in the *Belfast News Letter* on June 4-8, 1773.

Charlestown, January 15, 1773.

"For the Belfast News Letter.

We, the undernamed subscribers, think it is a duty incumbent upon us to acquaint the public in general and our friends in particular, that we went on board from Larne the ship Lord Dunluce, a stout commodious vessel, James Gillis, master; and after eleven weeks passage we arrived at Charlestown in South Carolina (our passage being prolonged by contrary winds, which beat us so far north, and continuing to blow from the south west, detained us near three weeks out of our way, notwithstanding all the care and unwearied diligence of our Captain, who did not fail

to take all safe advantage, in order to expedite our way).
But the tediousness of our voyage was rendered as agreeable to us as possible by the humane treatment of our
worthy captain, and agreeable company, together with the
useful and timely admonitions of our respected friends,
the Revd. William Martin, who never failed when the
weather and time would permit, to preach the everlasting
gospel to us, the which we esteemed a singular blessing.
We had plenty of provisions of good quality, and so
would have had as agreeable a passage, notwithstanding
the length of it, as any that ever was made from Ireland,
had it not happened that the smallpox broke out in the
vessel, which continued for some time, and occasioned
the death of some children; during which time our worthy
captain, and the Revd. Mr. Martin were duly employed
visiting the sick, and administering cordials to their several necessities etc., which disorders would have caused
us (according to the laws of the land) to have road quarantine six weeks, had not our captain, by his application
to a friend of his, through whose kind mediation we
obtained liberty to go ashore the day before the Grand
Court met, and got the favour of being called up to get our
warrants before those that had landed before with riding
fifteen days quarantine, which was a favour that not many
have been favoured with. Again, our worthy friend
Captain Gillis and Mr. Martin did not cease, at the expi-
ration of our voyage, to continue their fatherly care of us,
but used their utmost endeavours to obtain money to
carry us to our plantations, etc. Therefore we invite all
our friends that intend to come to this land, to sail with
Captain Gillis if possible, as he is both a solid, cautious,
and careful Captain as ever sailed in the passenger way;
the which opinion we were confirmed in by meeting with
some passengers who landed near the same time, and
hearing of their treatment, concluded that we would
rather pay Captain Gillis something extraordinary, than
sail with any other.

Signed: John Huey, Samuel Miller, Wm. Fairies, Charles Miller, John Craig, Wm. Humphrey, Archibald McWilliams, James Crawford, John Flemming, Richard Wright, James Sloan, Francis Adams, Wm. Adams, Wm. Miller, Samuel Barber, Hugh Owens, Wm. Greg, John Greg, James Brown, John Agnes, David Montgomery, John Baird, Alexander Fleming, Matthew Fleming, Wm. Crawford, Robert Reed, Abraham Thomson, Robert Hanna, Charles Burnit, John Roarke, John McQuillen, George Cherry, Thomas Weir, David McQuestin, James McQuestin, Wm. Barlow, Samuel Fear, Gilbert Menary, James McLurkin, Richard McLurken, Widow Mebin, Thomas McClurken, James Blair, Brice Blair, Thomas Wilson, David Murray and family, John McClenaghan, Archibald McNeel, James Wilson, Robert Jameson, John Henring.

During the period between 1750 and 1775 thousands of Scots-Irish people moved into South Carolina. Most were of Presbyterian stock, although some belonged to the Church of Ireland, the Society of Friends (Quakers) and the Irish Baptist movement. The Presbyterians were not all of the mainstream tradition – there were Covenanters, Seceders, Burghers, Anti-Burghers and Associates. It has been established that five Roman Catholics travelled from Ulster in the Martin party. The majority of the immigrants arrived in South Carolina under the "bounty" scheme. This entitlement of £4 was being offered to "poor Protestants" from Europe to settle in the region, with smaller amounts paid to children. The Scots-Irish were among those who availed generously of the bounty, but when the offer was abolished in 1768 the South Carolina authorities ruled that the settlers should be given lands free.

The Rev. William Martin and his Covenanting congregation from Ballymoney settled on the free lands, alongside members of the Seceders, a splinter Presbyterian group from neighbouring Ballyrashane, Derrykeghen and Kilraughts. Martin had received a call to South Carolina in 1770 and this may have influenced his decision to emigrate. With other Ulster settlers Martin's group combined to join a union church at Rocky Mountain Road, 15 miles from the town of

Chester. The inter-denominational Reformed church, formed in 1759, was named "Catholic" and Martin preached there for several years until his own Covenanting people withdrew and built their own log church on a spot two miles further on.

The Revolutionary War was being fought in America at the time and the Presbyterian settlers in South Carolina were caught up in the conflict. William Martin, conscious of the reasons he and his flock had to leave the north of Ireland, made clear from the pulpit his trenchant views on the British Tory colonial rulers.

Reminding his congregation of the hardships their fathers had endured in religion and in their possessions, he said: "They had been forced out of Ireland, had come over to America and cleared their lands and homes and their church and were free men". He warned that the British were coming in and soldiers would again be depriving them of the fruits of their labours, and would be driving them out. They should not stand, he said, meekly and idly by while all they had wrought was taken from them. "There was a time to pray and a time to fight and the time to fight had come", he said with deep conviction.

On the strength of this exhortation, two companies of militiamen were formed from the congregation, and the next day they set off with arms and horses to join the American revolutionary forces to repulse the British. William Martin's sermon, however, had reached the ears of British commanders and the church was burned down, he was arrested and confined to six months imprisonment. Martin was even brought before Lord Cornwallis to give an account of his activities, so notorious was his reputation with the British. On release Martin lived for a period in Mecklenburg County, a Scots-Irish Presbyterian stronghold in North Carolina, but after the British surrender at Yorktown he returned to Chester County and resumed charge of the "Catholic" congregation.

Two of William Martin's elders were Thomas McDill, who had arrived in Charleston in 1773 on the ship Pennsylvania Farmer, and David McQuestin, with the cleric on the ship Lord Dunluce in the same year.

A split occurred in 1782 when three Covenanting ministers, Cuthbertson, Dobbin and Lynn in Pennsylvania joined with other groups of Presbyterians to form the Associate Reformed Presbyterian Church. Martin stayed outside this grouping, claiming he was the only

Covenanter minister in America "who professed to teach the whole doctrine of the Reformation and who kept alive the Covenanter Church of America". By this time, William Martin had unfortunately taken to drink and in 1785 he was dismissed by the "Catholic" congregation for his "intemperance". Controversy raged on whether this fiery Ulsterman drunk to excess or whether he was merely accepted "treats" at various houses that he called on during visitations.

Writing in 1888, Chester County historian the Rev. Robert Latham said of William Martin: "It would have been regarded three-quarters of a century ago, as breach of the laws of civilised society for a parishioner not to have furnished his preacher with some kind of spirits when he came to visit him, either socially or ministerially. It was no doubt, when out visiting his Scotch-Irish neighbours, and enjoying their unbounded hospitality, that Mr. Martin became intoxicated. With all his faults or rather with this one fault, William Martin was a Christian gentleman and a patriot of the purest type. He made an impress for good at Rocky Creek which is felt to this day. His influence over the Covenanters was unbounded, and at his bidding they rose in their solid might to redeem what appeared to many, a lost cause".

His preaching continued, in school houses and in private homes, and it was said that his witness at that time did much to keep alive the Covenanting spirit on the frontier. In the early 1790s, he joined Reformed Church missionaries the Rev. James McGarragh, from Ireland, and the Rev. William King, from Scotland, in setting up a Reformed Presbytery. The alliance lasted only a few years, but Martin remained faithful to his own congregation at Rocky Mountain Road until his death in 1806, as a result of an injury by a fall from his horse. The faithful preacher was buried in a small graveyard near his cabin home. His epitaph read: "He was a large, fine looking man, a proficient scholar and eloquent preacher, and able divine".

Dr. George Howe's History of the Presbyterian Church in South Carolina provides some interesting information about the organisation of Catholic Church: "Tradition informs us that the white men were settled on Catawbe River near the mouth of some adventurous Indian traders quite in advance of the white population. In about 1751 or 52 there was an emigration from Pennsylvania of Scotch-Irish Presbyterians and also from Virginia, some of whom had formerly been of the Church of England. The progress of settlement was slow until 1755, when in consequence to Braddock's defeat in the French-Indian War and the incursion of the Indians, the whole country began to receive refugees from Pennsylvania and Virginia. These settlers opened communications with their friends in Ireland a direct immigration from that country which reached its height perhaps in 1768. Each man twenty-one years, or over, received a bounty grand of 100 acres of land, as a head right and an additional 50 acres for each member of his family. The principal inhabitants active in forming the congregation were Thomas Garrett, John Lee, Alexander McKeown and Hugh McDonald. The congregation was formed in 1759 by the labours of the Rev. William Richardson, who gave it the name of Catholic". Richardson was also to minister in the Waxhaws region of North Carolina.

The Rev. Robert Lathan, in his history of Union American Reformed Presbyterian Church, adds: "One of the oldest Presbyterian churches in Chester County is Catholic. At this place from May 1759 until 1773, Covenanters or Reformed Presbyterians, Associates and Presbyterians worshipped together".

Chester County became the stronghold of the Covenanting Presbyterian tradition in the South and the settlers needed real faith to survive in a region where hostile Indian tribes roamed freely. John McDonald, a brother of the first elder of Catholic Church, and his wife were killed by Cherokee Indians in 1761 and their children carried off as prisoners. The Catholic congregation was linked to a Reformed meeting house at nearby Hopewell, but they separated in 1788. William Martin had three wives: Mary and Jenny, who both died in Ireland before he emigrated, and the third Susanna, who survived him. He had one daughter.

William and Barbara Chestnut Moffatt were another typical Covenanting family from Co. Antrim who moved to South Carolina in the emigration wave of 1772. The Moffatts, with their young son Samuel, sailed from Belfast to Charleston on the Mary Jane ship and upon arrival were given 500 acres of land at Little Rock Creek in Chester County. William served in the Revolutionary army, maintaining a soldiering tradition of a forebear Samuel Mophet of Ayr in Scotland, who was involved in the battle of Bothwell's Bridge in the

Covenanter uprising of 1679. The Moffatts belonged to Ballylig Reformed Presbyterian Church in the parish of Rathcavin, which is located in the present-day Co. Antrim village of Broughshane.

The contribution of 65 revolutionary soldiers from Catholic Presbyterian Church at Chester County, South Carolina in the American War of Independence is recorded in a memorial at the church, unveiled in 1933. Almost all were first generation Ulster-Scots. Those who served were: Rev. William Martin, Capt. John Nixon, Capt. Hugh Knox, Samuel Adams, William Anderson, Robert Archer, John Bailey, John Bankhead, James Bankhead, James Barber, Joseph Barber, Hugh Boyd, John Brown Sr., John Caskey, George Caskey, George Crawford, Alexander Chestnut, Samuel Chestnut, Thomas Garrett, David Graham, James Graham, James Harbison, Patrick Harbison, William Harbison, Robert Harper, Andrew Hemphill, William Hicklin, Arthur Hicklin, James Jamieson, John Johnston, John King, James Knox, M.D., William Knox, John Land, Capt. John Steel, Capt. Benj. Land, John Lee, John Corder, David McCalla, Thomas McCalla, John McClurken, Matthew McClurken, Thomas McClurken, Hugh McDonald, William McDonald, William McGarity, Alexander McKown, James McKown, John McKown, Moses McKown, John McWaters, William Nesbit, James Peden, David Robinson, Thomas Stanford, William Starmount, Thomas Steel, William Stinson, Andrew Stevenson, William Stroud, Thomas Stroud, Hampton Stroud, John Stroud, Thomas Thorn.

Martin families from Ulster settled in the Abbeville district of South Carolina, some arriving via Charleston and others coming from Pennsylvania through Virginia. John Martin and his wife Sarah Dunn Martin were among early pioneers who founded the Presbyterian church out of which Erskine College at Due West later grew. Sarah was the daughter of Irish-born James Dunn, who was a distinguished Revolutionary War soldier.

11

Journey *to America* for four shillings and eight pence and the settlement of the Hearst family

Preacher and physician the Rev. Dr. Thomas Clark led 300 Presbyterians of the Seceder tradition from Ballybay in Co. Monaghan to America in May, 1764, landing at New York from Newry, Co. Down and settling at Stillwater (Salem). Clark, a Scotsman, had been minister of Ballybay (Cahans) Presbyterian Church from 1751 to 1764, and was well-known as an itinerant preacher in counties Monaghan, Tyrone, Down and Armagh.

The success of the Clark land settlements in America led New York councillor William Smith Jun. to encourage more movement of families from the Armagh-Monaghan-Tyrone region and he instructed William Cheevers, master of the sailing ship Needham, to recruit immigrants for a sailing from Newry on March 18, 1774. Cheevers went on an extensive tour through the region, visiting Monaghan, Castleblayney, Clones, Cootehill, Ballybay, Caledon, Armagh, Stewartstown and Dungannon and he enlisted 500 for the journey. About half of the number disembarked at New Castle, Delaware, the rest landed in New York. The cost of the passage was a mere four shillings and eight pence.

John Hearst was one of Dr. Thomas Clark's congregation who sailed in 1764 and with his son in 1776 settled on 500 acres of land at Long Cane in the up-country from Charleston in South Carolina close to Abbeville. John Hearst and his wife Elizabeth Knox had 11 children, several of the sons serving in the Revolutionary War – John Jun. as a major and Joseph as a private. John Hearst Jun. married Martha

Carson and most of their 10 children moved westward. A third son, George, left South Carolina in 1808 for a homestead at Meramec in Missouri and he prospered with his two sons, William G. and Joseph, in livestock production and mining. William G. Hearst married Elizabeth Collins in 1817 and their first son George was named after his South Carolina pioneer grandfather. The family was then the most prosperous in the region with 120 acres of land.

George Hearst went to California in the gold rush, made his fortune, and became a senator for the sunshine state in 1886-91. His only son, William Randolph Hearst, was a member of Congress from New York and founder of Hearst Publishing, becoming one of America's most famous journalists.

George's interest in mining was inspired by the prospectors his father hired to work claims on the family land. After limited schooling, he studied mining at the Franklin County Mining School in 1838. He is remembered by neighbours as "a raw country youth of 19 who tramped the hills and hollows barefooted."

In November 1844, William G. Hearst died, leaving widow, Elizabeth; daughter, Martha; and two sons, George and Jacob. Hearst's will described Jacob as "rendered helpless by disease" and made provisions for his care and support. In less than two years Jacob also was dead. In 1848 Elizabeth Collins Hearst remarried, to a postmaster and former county judge, Joseph Funk. A year later, news of the California gold strikes reached Missouri, and George was no longer content managing the family land and other business holdings. He bade farewell to his family and headed west. Six women and eight other men, including his cousins, Joseph and James Clark, comprised the overland group.

Dread of Indians and fear of sickness were uppermost in the minds of those on the California trail. Although Hearst avoided difficulty with the Indians, he did contract a severe case of cholera. Chills, insatiable thirst, stomach pains, cramped legs and diarrhoea halted his horse-back progress after about a month on the trail. He became separated from his cousins and the rest of the original Missouri party, who were forced to continue without him. Hearst recovered sufficiently to be able to mount his horse and ride, although he was still quite ill and after several days of hard travel, he rejoined the Missourians.

They resumed their journey and six months out of Missouri arrived at the South Fork of California's American River. Hearst and his companions headed first for Diamond Springs, then to Hangtown and finally on to Jackass Gulch, where recent promising strikes had been made. The entire winter's work resulted in only small return. Hearst and his cousins abandoned their claim in the spring of 1851, he and the Clarks realised they would never be millionaires by washing gold in that unyielding granite canyon. For the next seven years, George Hearst continued to stake claims throughout the northern California gold fields.

In 1858 his stepfather, Joseph Funk, sent news of George's Missouri properties and asked him to return home to visit his aging mother. Hearst responded by sending 300 dollars to his mother, writing: "My chances are pretty good to make money at present .... If the claim ... holds out as it has so far, it is one of the good things that is sometimes found in California." As for his return, he wrote to his stepfather, "I would like to see you and mother ... much better than you suppose, but to come home without money is out of the question; but if I have any kind of luck I will come home soon and stop awhile, thought I do not expect to make Missouri my home; I am satisfied I could not stand that climate."

George prospected on the western slope of the Sierra until July 1859, when the Comstock Lode was discovered near the present town of Carson City, Nevada. George Hearst and his friends travelled east over the Sierra on pack mules, part of the "great backward rush from California." Although the Comstock mining area had been prospected by gold miners for 10 years with some success, Hearst was one of the first to examine the "heavy black stuff" that clogged the mining pans and rockers. While the other miners believed that the black ore was lead and discarded it, Hearst thought it might be silver. he quickly staked a claim named the Ophir.

By March, 1860, almost 10 years after leaving Missouri, George Hearst realised $80,000 from his mine. He bought another claim, the Gould & Curry, to add to his original Ophir holdings, A new mining camp, Virginia City, sprang up as Hearst's and other miners' claims paid handsomely. Hearst invested a portion of his new fortune in other mines, banked another portion and then decided to make his long-awaited trip back to Missouri to see his mother, then very low with consumption. She died seven months later.

George, now in his forties, married Phoebe Elizabeth Apperson, the 18-year-old daughter of a prosperous Missouri family, who could trace their roots back to Ulster-born pair David Hanson, from Co. Londonderry, and Sidney Major Hanson, from Co. Antrim. The Hansons, who were linen weavers and Presbyterians, sailed from Belfast in 1796 and settled in Virginia and South Carolina before moving to Missouri.

The Hearst interest in mining continued after George moved back to California in 1862 with his young wife.

William Randolph Hearst was born in 1863 and his formative years were spent mainly with his mother as his father was continually away on mining business in Utah, Nevada, the Dakotas and Arizona. Through his wealth George Hearst gained much political influence in the Democratic Party and a $100,000 donation helped found the San Francisco newspaper, *The Examiner*.

George Hearst was elected for a six-year term in the US Senate, beginning in March, 1887. William Randolph, his son, retained his original enthusiasm for the newspaper business in general and the San Francisco Examiner in particular. However, George was still unconvinced that journalism was a suitable career, but he relented and deeded ownership of the newspaper to his son.

On the same day George Hearst was sworn into office as a United States senator from California, his son began a 65-year career in journalism with an announcement on an inside page of the March 4, 1887 issue of the San Francisco paper: "The Examiner, with this issue, has become the exclusive property of William R. Hearst, son of its former proprietor: It will be conducted in the future on the same lines and policies which characterised its career under the control of Senator Hearst."

The Hearst publishing dynasty was beginning in earnest, a far cry from the humble settlement at Abbeville in South Carolina.

John Whitewell Hearst, a son of John Jun., remained in Abbeville and two of his sons had distinguished service for the Confederacy in the Civil War. Rifleman Joseph Lewis Hearst lost an arm in the Second

Battle of the Manassas (Bull Run) in Virginia, while his brother John Thomas Jefferson Hearst was a lieutenant in the cavalry at various battles and was in Virginia when General Robert E. Lee surrendered. As part of the surrender terms, Confederate officers were allowed to keep a horse to return home and John Thomas Jefferson Hearst allowed his soldiers to take turns at riding his horse, as many had no boots and their feet were wrapped in rags. In their various settlements in America, the Hearsts remained active Presbyterians, a number of them associating with the Reformed Covenanting tradition.

The Heards were another Ulster family who settled in the Long Cane area close to Abbeville after moving from Lancaster County in Pennsylvania and Albemarle in Virginia. They had first emigrated from Co. Tyrone about 1720 – brothers Stephen and Charles Heards – and their farming/blacksmith skills were put to good use on the frontier. Second and third generation of the Heards extended into Virginia, Georgia, North Carolina, Tennessee and South Carolina, with sons and grandsons carrying on the family trade as blacksmiths. They also served as militiamen in the Revolutionary War.

From Co. Tyrone to Pennsylvania and Abbeville in South Carolina also came the Pettigrews, a Presbyterian family with distinguished service in the wars in both Ireland and America. The original James Pettigrew, a Huguenot Protestant, came from France to Scotland prior to 1648 and commanded a troop of horses under Oliver Cromwell. His son James II Pettigrew settled at Crilley near Dungannon in Co. Tyrone in 1660 and for valour under King William the Third at the Battle of the Boyne in 1690 he received a grant of 380 acres of land.

James II married Martha Moore, from Scotland, and they had six sons and three daughters. James died aged 93 and his son James III, born at Crilley in 1713, landed at New Castle, Delaware in 1740. He first settled in Philadelphia with his wife Mary Cochran, from Grange, Armagh, and the extent of his prosperity can be gauged by the fact that he had five hundred pounds on arrival in America.

In 1773, James III Pettigrew bought a farm at Abbeville in South Carolina, about 10 miles up from his first home in the region at Long Cane Creek. He served with the colonial troops in the Revolutionary Army. His son John Pettigrew was another Abbeville citizen of note and he is recorded as having been paid for both duty as horseman and foot soldier in the American Revolution.

A frontier parody *revealed the hopes and aspirations of the Scots-Irish pioneer*

"*Droop not, brother, as we go*
Over the mountains, westward ho,
Under boughs of mistletoe,
Log huts we'll rear,
While herds of deer and buffalo
Furnish the cheer;
File over the mountains, steady, boys;
For game afar
We have our rifles ready, boys,
Aha-a-a-a-a-a!

Cheer up , brothers, as we go
Over the mountains, westward ho!
When we've wood and prairie land
Won by our toil,
We'll reign like kings in the fairyland
Lords of the soil,
Then westward ho in legions, boys,
For freedom's star
Points to her sunset regions, boys,
Aha-a-a-a-a-a!"

- **From the collection of the late Victor Barringer**

12

'Poor Calvinists' *in Williamsburg*

The oldest inland settlement in South Carolina is Kingstree, today the main township of Williamsburg County. There, in 1732 "poor Calvinists" from the north of Ireland sailed up Black River from Charleston to build day shelters around the King's Tree, a white pine on the banks of the river. Williamsburg township, from which Kingstree grew, was named after William III, the Dutch King who secured the Protestant succession in Britain with his victory over Roman Catholic monarch James II at the Battle of the Boyne in Ireland in July 1690.

The Scots-Irish settlers in Williamsburg were of Covenanting Presbyterian stock, who had moved from Drumbo and Knockbracken in Co. Down near the shores of Belfast Lough. They included the Witherspoons, Armstrongs, Wilsons and Friersons, families, who for almost 50 years, were to become known in South Carolina records as "the poor Protestants".

In the first year of their settlement, they were given provisions by the Council of South Carolina. This included Indian corner, rice, wheat, flour, beef, pork, rum and salt. Each hand over 16 years of age was furnished with an axe and a brood and narrow hoe – tools of the land. The first Presbyterian church organised in the Carolina back country was set up at Williamsburg in 1836, with John Witherspoon as the main inspiration at the log meeting house on the two-acre site. Witherspoon was said to be a man "well versed" in the scriptures and the principles of Presbyterianism.

The first Williamsburg settlers faced horrendous physical, spiritual and environmental difficulties and in the great influenza epidemic of 1749, 80 of the immigrant community died. There had also been famine resulting in many deaths and in desperation some of the men from Williamsburg trekked to North Carolina for food.

The Scots-Irish families at Williamsburg were among the most enthusiastic for the revolutionary cause during the War of Independence and four companies were recruited to fight the British. William Frierson had five sons who served as soldiers, with one Major John Frierson, recorded for gallantry in the War Department at Washington. Few Williamsburg residents held public office before the Revolution. This was the preserve of those giving allegiance to the Anglican Church. The Presbyterian Covenanters from Ulster made few bows to the Episcopacy.

The first Williamsburg Presbyterians were a conservative people, who tightly maintained the constitution and discipline of their Calvinist church. The Sabbath was strictly kept and sinners stood trial and were censured if found guilty. The church was the religious, judicial and social centre of the community.

When a fresh influx of Scots-Irish settlers arrived in the region about 1770, schisms developed in the church as more liberal theological doctrines were propagated. In 1782, the Rev. Samuel Kennedy arrived from Ireland to occupy the Williamsburg pulpit and his liberal theology, which, it is claimed, included the "denial" of the Divinity of Christ, deepened the split. The conservatives withdrew to form a separate congregation, known as Bethel, but the bitterness continued to the point that on an August night in 1786, the old church was raised to the ground. The split was now irrevocable and friction continued for several decades. In March, 1805, four families from the original settlements headed on a 600-mile trek westwards in covered wagons to lush new lands in the Franklin/ Columbia region of Maury County in middle Tennessee. Within a year the Armstrong, Friersons, Blakeleys and Fultons were joined in Tennessee by 10 additional families – the Dickeys, Flemings, Witherspoons, Stephensons and more Friersons, and by their beloved pastor, the Rev. James White Stephenson and doctor Samuel Mayes.

They settled on eight square miles, 5,000 acres of lush, highly productive acreage that was for centuries Indian hunting grounds. The land was purchased from the heirs of General Nathaniel Greene, a part of the 25,000 acres in Maury County granted to him for services in the Revolutionary War. The purchase price was 15,360 dollars.

Outside the town of Columbia, where Presidents James Knox Polk and Andrew Johnson and Davy Crockett and Sam Houston launched their political careers, the Williamsburg families established Zion Presbyterian Church on traditional Covenanting principles and the Lord's Supper was celebrated for the first time there in August 1809 with 54 communicants.

• Kingstree in South Carolina has a population today of close on 3,000. Decendants of its first Scots-Irish and Huguenot settlers there remain "inveterate" hunters and anglers in a picturesque region of forests and lakes.

• Drumbo and Knockbracken are situated in the Greater Belfast area, forming part of the boroughs of Castlereagh and Lisburn. The Presbyterian tradition remains very strong in this predominantly Protestant part of Northern Ireland. Covenanting Presbyterians in Northern Ireland today belong to the Reformed Presbyterian Church of Ireland, a denomination that exists separate from the mainstream Presbyterian Church in Ireland and is strongest in Counties Antrim and Down.

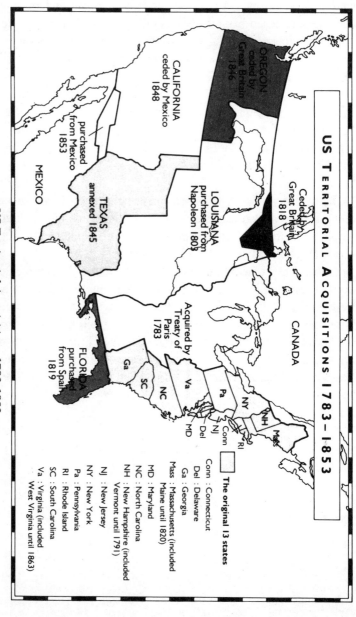

US Territorial Acquisitions 1783-1853

13

The Moores *of Walnut Grove*
and heroine Kate Barry

Walnut Grove plantation in Spartanburg County, South Carolina was the centrepoint of one of the most progressive settlements of the Scots-Irish on the American frontier in the 18th century. It was there that Ulster-born teacher Charles Moore extended his considerable knowledge obtained through a university education back in Ireland and the family became an illustrious name in the region long after his death in 1805.

Charles Moore and his wife Mary Barry were of lowland Scottish Presbyterian stock whose families had lived in Co. Antrim for upwards of a century before the couple emigrated to America about 1750. A kinsman William Moore was said to have defended Londonderry for the Protestant cause during the historic siege of 1688-89. The Moores came to Pennsylvania with 13 other Ulster families: Barrys, Andersons, Collins, Thomsons, Vernons, Pearsons, Jamisons, Dodds, Rays, Penneys, McMahons, Nichols and Millers and later when they moved to the South Carolina Piedmont region around Spartanburg they became known as the Tyger River colonies.

These families moved southwards along the Great Wagon Road from Pennsylvania through the Shenandoah Valley of Virginia, into North Carolina at Anson/Rowan counties and eventually, over a period of almost a decade, they settled on the western edge of the South Carolina frontier.

Charles Moore was a dominant spirit in this community and being a professional man he had no difficulty in obtaining a land grant, courtesy of King George III in England. The original grant of 500 acres on the banks of the North Tyger River in 1763 was eventually developed to 3,000 acres on what was a very pleasant, highly productive environment, compared to the vagaries of life and climate back in the north of Ireland.

Buffalo roamed the green meadows and cane brakes in their hundreds, wild turkeys abounded and for the hunter there were also deer, elk, bear and panthers in great abundance. The land was naturally very rich in soil and plant. It had been a region where Cherokee Indian tribes had come to hunt, fish and make their cooking vessels from soapstone, a substance not unlike granite.

Charles Moore was listed in a 1762 deed of Anson County, North Carolina as a schoolmaster and his reputation as a pioneering teacher on the frontier was known far and wide. The Anson/Rowan region of North Carolina had been settled by Scots-Irish families from the late 1740s/early 1750s and Moore lived there until after the Indian wars had subsided and it was considered safe to move down to what is today Spartanburg County. The Moores brought to the extensive settlement they were to call Walnut Grove six children, five daughters and a son. Two sons were later born at the plantation.

At Spartanburg, Charles Moore taught his three sons and several dozen children of the other families who had trekked down from North Carolina. The school was known as Rocky Springs and there Moore taught elementary and secondary lessons in English, Latin, spelling and mathematics. Only boys were allowed to attend school – girls had domestic duties to perform with mother in the home. The school schedule had its breaks for barnraising, husking bees, harvesting and the many chores associated with farmlands on the frontier.

Charles Moore had been involved in the earliest school in Spartanburg County, known as Eustatie Academy. It had been founded in 1765 by the trustees of Nazareth Presbyterian Church and from this school emerged the Moore seat of learning at Rocky Springs. The Nazareth congregation, organised in 1765, had pledged to "secure the best education possible for their children and for the promotion of the general interest of education throughout the state". Education was the watchword for frontier Presbyterians.

Andrew Barry Moore, Charles Moore's ninth child, moved from his father's one-room school to Dickinson College at Carlisle,

Pennsylvania, travelling on horse back for studies. He graduated in medicine and practised in the Spartanburg County for more than 40 years. For more than a decade, Andrew Barry Moore served in the South Carolina house of representatives and was US postmaster for Walnut Grove.

An elder brother Thomas Moore was also a member of the South Carolina house of representatives, and was a Congressman in the United States house of representatives at Washington. He had fought in the Revolutionary War at Cowpens and other battles and was a major general in the War of 1812 and 1815, in charge of the defence of the South Carolina coast. Charles Moore Jun., the youngest of the family, was postmaster at Walnut Grove, but moved to Perry County in Alabama in 1830 and a son Andrew Barry Moore was Governor of Alabama in 1857-65.

Charles Moore died in 1805, a year after his wife Mary. His obituary in the Charleston City Gazette described him as "an outstanding citizen" – parent, master, neighbour and benefactor. The seven Moore daughters – Margaret Catherine, Alice, Rosa, Mary, Rachel, Violet and Elizabeth – were all formidable women for the times, none more so than the eldest Margaret Catherine (Kate) whose fame was spread abroad for the heroinism she displayed during the Revolutionary War. Kate's birth in 1752 has not been positively identified as being in Ireland, Pennsylvania or North Carolina, but there was no doubting her indomitable Scots-Irish character. She was made of stern stuff as was proved when she emerged as a Revolutionary heroine at the Battle of Cowpens in 1781.

Family history relates that when she was young, Kate was given some walnuts to bake a cake. She planted a few that were left over and they grew to become a grove, Walnut Grove, the name Charles Moore gave his plantation. The proximity to the Tyger River provided ample supplies of water for livestock and healthy drinking water for family requirements. The United States census of 1790 showed Walnut Grove plantation to have nine black slaves.

Kate Moore was only 15 in 1767 when she married Captain Andrew Barry, who was also from a Scots-Irish family. Andrew's birthplace in 1744, like Kate's has not been positively identified and historians list either Ireland or Pennsylvania. He was a magistrate of the Crown in South Carolina until the Revolutionary War broke out in 1775 and was one of the first elders of Nazareth Presbyterian Church. Andrew Barry and his two brothers Richard and John had come to Spartanburg County in 1762 and Richard married Rosa Moore, Kate's sister. John Barry married Rebecca McCord, moved to Tennessee, then Kentucky. His son Senator William Taylor Barry was President Andrew Jackson's Postmaster General in the White House and fought in the War of 1812-13. He was also US Minister to Spain.

Andrew Barry enlisted on the Revolutionary side early in the War and served as a captain in the partisan rangers under his brother-in-law Colonel Thomas Moore. He was in command of companies at the battles of Fishing Creek, Musgrove's Mill (where he was wounded) and Cowpens. Kate and he settled across the Tyger River, about two miles from Walnut Grove. They had 11 children, five sons and six daughters.

South Carolina folklore about Kate Barry's role in the Revolutionary War abounds and she is remembered as one of the great heroines on the American patriot side. She acted as a volunteer scout and guide for the patriots of the Carolina Piedmont area, always in support of her husband. Her scouting operations centred mainly in Spartanburg County and being an excellent horse woman, able to ride side saddle, she was familiar with the thick wooded wilderness and Indian trails.

Kate frequently rode to where the patriots were camped to warn of impending danger. She had an ally in the black slave, Uncle Cato, who, when it was impossible for her to go on scouting expeditions, stepped into the breach. Kate and Uncle Cato would fill hollow trees with corn to provide against emergencies. Raids by the British forces sometimes left patriot families destitute and the corn caches in the trees were needed to feed the people and their animals. The dangers were many for Kate Barry, who was even engaged in rounding up militia troops when reinforcements were needed. At the battle of Cowpens in January, 1781 she played this role to good effect when at one stage all seemed lost for the patriots in the face of oncoming British forces. Kate Barry, in her voluntary assignment as scout for General Daniel Morgan, gathered up patriot bands and moved them to the battle front. There, her husband was holding the line with General Andrew Pickens against troops under renowned British commander Banastre Tarleton, a Liverpudlian despised by the frontier settlers for his butchery.

During the battle of Cowpens the women of Nazareth Presbyterian Church, 13 miles away, were assembled at a house near the church and the ever watchful Kate was at the shoals on Tyger River, waiting for reports from the battle. When informed of the crushing victory for the patriots she rushed to the women with the news. The reversal at Cowpens was a big blow to the British. An estimated 926 of Tarleton's troops were killed, captured or wounded and many armaments were taken. On the American side only 12 were killed, 60 wounded. It was to be the forerunner to final British humiliation at Yorktown.

Tradition recounts how, when the Tories under "Bloody Bill" Cunningham made their infamous raid into her area, Kate heard them from across the river near her father's house. Tying her two-year-old daughter, Catherine (Little Katie) to the bed post for safety, she rode to her husband's company for help and this forced the Tories to retreat. More than 200 years on, she is still widely acclaimed in the Carolinas as the "heroine of the battle of the Cowpens."

Once, the Tories came to Kate's house demanding to have information on the whereabouts of her husband's company. She refused to give this, was tied up and struck three times with a leash. This incident angered the men of her husband's company and it was said any one of them would have given his own life to save hers.

After the war, Major Crawford, a mutual friend, said to Andrew Barry, "It's your duty to kill Elliott, the Tory, who struck Margaret Barry with a whip. But if you will not, then I will kill him, for no man shall be allowed to live who struck Margaret Barry". Andrew then went with 10 men to find Elliott, and became so enraged that he picked up a stool and struck Elliott senseless to the floor. He then said, "I am satisfied, I will not take his life."

In another incident, with the British in hot pursuit, Kate swam her horse across the Pacolet River near Hurricane Shoals. Miraculously the water rose to a high level just as she and her horse reached dry ground on the other side, thus preventing the British from capturing her and the important news she carried.

Andrew Barry died in 1811. Kate outlived him by 13 years and in 1823 she died at the age of 71 and was buried at Walnut Grove. Her tombstone reads, "Sacred to the memory of our mother, Margaret Barry, who departed this life September 29, 1823, aged 71 years." She left a short will, which is on file at the Spartanburg County Courthouse. Her direct descendants are to be found in South Carolina, Georgia, and Alabama but principally in Mississippi.

Colonel Thomas John Moore, a grandson of Charles and Mary Moore, served in the South Carolina House of Representatives and Senate. He was a Confederate Army officer in the Civil War, serving with the 18th South Carolina Volunteers in the Carolinas and Virginia. He was imprisoned by forces after capture in 1865 and held until the War ended. After a pardon issued by President Andrew Johnson, Thomas Moore was appointed colonel in the 36th regiment of the South Carolina state militia. In civilian life, Colonel Moore was devoted to agricultural pursuits and was a state senator for four years.

Thomas Moore Craig Jun., a great-great-great grandson of Charles and Mary Moore, also had a spell, in 1972-74, in the South Carolina House of Representatives. With other Moore descendants, he still maintains an interest in the Walnut Grove plantation.

The Craig connection with the Moores of Walnut Grove dates back to James Craig, who was born at Templepatrick, Co. Antrim in 1754 and arrived at Charleston in 1773 on board the ship Britannia. In 1777 James married Jinny Bell, born at Ahoghill, Co. Antrim in 1758. Their son Arthur Rosborough Craig married Henrietta Sue Moore, great-grandaughter of Charles and Mary Moore.

• In 1961, Walnut Grove plantation was given by Thomas Moore Craig Jun. and his family to the Spartanburg County Historical Association. The property is today held in trust as a public amenity by the Spartanburg County Foundation.

14

From Co. Antrim *to Fairview,*
South Carolina

Fairview, the first Presbyterian Church in Greenville County, South Carolina was established in 1786 by three families who had emigrated from Co. Antrim – the Pedens, the Alexanders and the Nesbits. John and Peggy McDill Peden left Co. Antrim in 1773, settling initially in Spartanburg, South Carolina with their seven sons and three daughters. They were a God-fearing family. John had been a ruling elder in his church back in Ulster and when the family placed their roots on Carolina soil their immediate task was to erect a place of worship.

In the rugged, open highland country they organised the Nazareth Presbyterian Church near Spartanburg and the simple log meeting house was the scene of frequent attacks by hostile Cherokee Indian tribes, which led to the deaths of a number of the settlers. After the Revolutionary War, John and Peggy McDill Peden moved to Chester in South Carolina, but sons John, Samuel and David, along with James Alexander and James Nesbit, purchased land at Greenville and settled there. James Alexander donated a site for a church near his home and the families named it Fairview after their congregation in Co. Antrim.

The first ruling elders of the church were John and Samuel Peden and John Alexander, and the first sermon was preached by the Rev. Samuel Edmondson on April 10, 1787. Edmondson had a licence from the Hanover Presbytery in Virginia in 1733, as part of the 'New Side' revival which grew out of the 'Great Awakening' in America.

The first regular minister at Fairview was the Rev. John McCosh, another born in Co. Antrim. He also served in Rocky Springs and Liberty Springs Presbyterian Churches in South Carolina and tradition states that he taught the wife of an elder of Rocky Springs how to prepare the Communion bread. He never married, and during his time at Fairview he was assisted in the ministry by the Rev. Robert McClintock.

McCosh was succeeded in 1794 by Pennsylvania-born the Rev. James Templeton and a later pastor in the congregation was the Rev. Alexander Kirkpatrick, from Ballymena in Co. Antrim. He served only two years (1817-18) and it was said of him: "This fair, fat rosy Irishman was a favourite with the younger members of the congregation, while the elders did not think him sufficiently sedate. To their jibes he returned the reply – 'only a Christian has the right to be happy'." Another Ulsterman, the Rev. Thomas D. Baird had a three-year ministry at Fairview after Kirkpatrick.

The Pedens, Alexanders and Nesbits had been allocated lands in the Fairview section of Greenville county in recognition of military service in the Revolutionary War and when they moved from Spartanburg County in 1786 their deeds, and their Bibles, were their most cherished possessions.

Records vividly describe the journey to Greenville: "Nightfall found us footsore and weary beside a cold spring of ice cold water issuing from among rocks and the roots of an immense tulip or poplar tree. Here in this green spot the tired guides kindled the first campfire to have a cheery blaze when the others came up the stream. Before they allowed themselves to partake of food or indulge in rest, the Peden brothers – John, Samuel and David – retired apart on the eastern hillside and joined hands in solemn covenant with God and each other. After prayer they repeated a Psalm and, singing Old Hundredth, went down to camp. After a simple meal of Indian corn porridge, known as 'mush', and milk hastily drawn from the few cows and cooled in the spring, they sang a hymn, had a prayer and laid down to sleep under the star-studded canopy of heaven."

James Alexander Sen., who gave the land where Fairview church, cemetery and session houses were built, was born in Co. Antrim in 1725 and died at Fairview in 1810. His memorial tribute reads: "He was the first magistrate of Fairview and as large hearted and open handed a colonialist. as the old world ever furnished the new – the mastermind and pivot on which the settlement of Fairview turned".

The first two Fairview meeting houses were log-built, the third, erected in 1818 was made of brick. When the first families arrived, the region was very densely forested and logs were the obvious materials for their homes and churches. The third church was described as "a large brick barn with a very square roof without gables and an outside stairway leading to the gallery used for colored members". The Fairview settlers had slaves. The seats or pews were arranged in tiers or terraces of four, down from the doors to the pulpit. Above the pulpit hung the sounding board, resembling an open umbrella or huge wooden toadstool. The boxed-up pulpit was so small and high with steps so steep and narrow that a visiting minister once gave great offence by remarking: "Satan must have planned this pulpit".

Church attendance during the first years of the Fairview settlement were obligatory. If absence was unexplained, the elders visited the members to determine the reason. Services were held twice a month for many years as the minister or supply minister was shared with other congregations. Temporal matters relating to the financial needs of the church were taken care of on the Saturday. Elders also exercised discipline of members accused of "drunkenness, fighting, quarrelling at muster, stealing, adultery and breach of the Sabbath". A collection was not uplifted at Fairview services until 1867. Services were long, held in the morning and afternoon, with a recess for dinner. Each family provided food for its own, with sufficient for visitors in attendance. The worshippers came from a wide area – on foot, horseback and by gig, buggy or carriage.

At communion services, a member was required to present a "token" before being allowed to partake of the sacraments of the bread and wine. These "tokens", pewter or lead coins, were given to members if they answered satisfactorily questions asked by the elders prior to Communion. The practice was discontinued in the 1840s.

The north west section of South Carolina around Greenville and Spartanburg was the last portion of the state to be surrendered by the Cherokee Indians and in 1777 a treaty signed by the then Governor Glenn, opened up the region to the incoming settlers, many of them Scots-Irish families who landed at Charleston.

Reedy River Baptist was the oldest established church in the Greenville area, founded in 1777; Lebanon Methodist was set up at Fork Shoals in 1785 and a year later Fairview Presbyterian took root. The Nazareth Presbyterian Church near Spartanburg where the Pedens originally worshipped was organised in 1772. Scots-Irish families had been in the region since the late 1750s, meeting for worship in homes. From 1765 they used a log meeting house for services. Another Scots-Irish group from Pennsylvania and Virginia settled along the banks of the Tyger River in the north west part of South Carolina in 1761.

This was Cherokee Indian hunting ground and the first permanent settlement in what is now Spartanburg County was formed by a group of Scots-Irish Presbyterian families who came from Pennsylvania to the Tyger River territory. Another group came from Ireland by way of Charleston.

The settlers of the Tyger River rode horseback, walked miles and even waded across streams to attend worship. Danger of attack from Indians was in the air as the men stacked their rifles and ammunition pouches in a pile except those who stood guard while the minister preached to the congregation. Bricks for the original Nazareth Church were made on the river banks and sun-dried on the nearby hillside. The original floor was made of large square bricks, the high pulpit was on the side near the cemetery and the pews were made of heart pine.

Nazareth Church was formally organised in 1772 by the Rev. Joseph Alexander and the first ruling elders were Robert Nesbit, John McElrath, Andrew Barry and Thomas Peden. The Nazareth cemetery is one of the oldest in the South Carolina up-country, with many Revolutionary soldiers buried there.

The original Nazareth church families were Barry, Moore, Anderson, Collins, Thompson, Vernon, Pearson, Jamison, Dodd, Ray, Penney, McMahon, Nicholls, and Miller. These were known as the Pennsylvania Irish, as they emigrated first to that State, and from there to South Carolina. Several years afterwards, in 1767, or 1768, a second colony came directly from Ireland through Charleston, principally from County Antrim. The first colony settled on the Tyger rivers, the second on the highlands adjoining. The second colony consisted of the families of Coan, Snoddy, Peden, Alexander, Gaston and Morton. When finally settled the two colonies covered a territory nearly twenty miles square.

Dr. George Howe, in his 'History of the Presbyterian Church in South Carolina,' said of the Nazareth Congregation: "They were full of reverence for God's Word, and for the institutions of religion, and no sooner had they established their homes in the new world, than they made the best arrangements in their power for the worship of the God of their fathers".

It is said that every able-bodied man of the Nazareth congregation fought for American independence. They were at the battles of Kings Mountain, Cowpens, Charleston, Yorktown, Valley Forge and Ninety Six. Between battles these farmers and part-time soldiers were allowed to return to their homes for the protection of their families and, when they were needed, the word was spread quickly from neighbour to neighbour. They formed the Spartan Regiment, from which Spartanburg got its name, and it was said the Scots-Irish womenfolk showed "as much fortitude in suffering and hardship as the men displayed in fighting".

Tragedy struck the congregation in 1780-83 with a number of violent deaths. John Caldwell, a lad of 14, was killed by Tory loyalists when he went to warn neighbours of their approach. John Snoddy and Captain Steadman died in separate incidents, while William Anderson was murdered in a tomahawk attack. The Anderson home was burned, but his wife escaped and walked six miles to safety in the darkness, crossing two rivers. There was also the accidental killing of Patrick Crawford by his friend Thomas Moore, who mistook him for an enemy soldier on a scouting expedition.

This was a violent period in the Carolina up-country, but the Nazareth and Fairview congregations prospered and today they are still actively witnessing for the faith.

The Southern States of America

ALABAMA
Capital: Montgomery
Area: 131,485 sq km (50,766 sq miles)
Population: 4,040,600

ARKANSAS
Capital: Little Rock
Area: 134,880 sq km (52,077 sq miles)
Population: 2,350,800

FLORIDA
Capital: Tallahassee
Area: 140,255 sq km (54,152 sq miles)
Population: 12,938,000

GEORGIA
Capital: Atlanta
Area: 150,365 sq km (58,056 sq miles)
Population: 6,478,300

LOUISIANA
Capital: Baton Rouge
Area: 115,310 sq km (44,521 sq miles)
Population: 4,220,000

MISSISSIPPI
Capital: Jackson
Area: 122,335 sq km (47,233 sq miles)
Population: 2.573.300

NORTH CAROLINA
Capital: Raleigh
Area: 126,505 sq km (48,843 sq miles)
Population: 6,628,700

SOUTH CAROLINA
Capital: Columbia
Area: 78,225 sq km (30,202 sq miles)
Population: 3,486,700

TENNESSEE
Capital: Nashville
Area: 106,590 sq km (41,154 sq miles)
Population: 4,877,200

TEXAS
Capital: Austin
Area: 678,620 sq km (262,017 sq miles)
Population: 16,986,500

15

The formidable *John C. Calhoun*

John Caldwell Calhoun – one of the most influential statesmen and politicians in the American south during the first half of the 19th century – was a second generation Ulsterman who literally hauled himself up from his bootlaces. This son of a Scots-Irish merchant and trader, Patrick Calhoun, rose to become American Vice-President to John Quincy Adams (1825-29) and Andrew Jackson (1829-32), yet remarkably he was self-taught until the age of 18 in the humble log-cabined settlements of the South Carolina back ground around Abbeville. Patrick Calhoun had emigrated with his family from Londonderry to Pennsylvania in 1733 when he was just six.

Under the tuition of his brother-in-law the Rev. Moses Waddell, John C. Calhoun gained the early grounding in life which enabled him later to graduate from Yale and study law at Litchfield in Connecticut. He was elected to the South Carolina state legislator in 1807 and to the American Congress in 1810 on "hawkish" policies of the nationalist wing of Thomas Jefferson's party. With a political contemporary Henry Clay, Calhoun stirred up patriotic feelings for the war with Britain in 1812.

Calhoun's resignation from Congress in 1817 allowed him to become Secretary of War under President James Monroe until 1825 and during this period his Presidential ambitions were fuelled. He had, however, to be content with an eight-year stint as Vice-President, first to John Quincy Adams and second to Andrew Jackson. In a disagreement with Jackson, Calhoun resigned as Vice-President, the only man to do so until 1973 when Spiro Agnew was forced to stand down under very different circumstances.

He strongly opposed the abolition of slavery and strenuously worked to defend the rights of the states, particularly his own South Carolina homeland. He served in the state legislature, congress and senate for more than 40 years. In two books he wrote in the 1840s, 'Disquisition of Government' and 'A Discourse on the Constitution and Government of the United States', Calhoun set out a conservative political philosophy that was to become a watermark for many across the nation.

John C. Calhoun was born in 1782 by his Donegal-born father Patrick's second wife Martha Caldwell, who was Virginian-born of Scots-Irish immigrant parents from Co. Antrim. Patrick's first wife was Jane Craighead, who died in 1766 after giving birth to twins. The family experienced extreme hardships in the early years in South Carolina, and death at the hands of Indian tribes. Patrick Calhoun Sen., the first emigrant, was 49 when he moved from Convoy, Raphoe, Co. Donegal in 1733 with his family, settling in Pennsylvania before setting up home at Albemarl County in Virginia. He died in 1741. His wife Catherine Montgomery Calhoun was born in Londonderry in 1683 and after her husband's death she moved to Abbeville County, South Carolina in 1756, where she was to die in the Indian massacre at Long Cane on February 1, 1760.

Patrick Calhoun Jun., a Covenanting Presbyterian, organised the Hopewell Presbyterian congregation (first known as Lower Long Cane Church) near Abbeville in 1760 and worshippers carried muskets in case of Indian attack. As the minister there preached he held a gun in his hand and a powder horn suspended from his shoulder, such was the danger abroad.

The Long Cane Massacre on February 1, 1760 occurred as 150 settlers, mostly Scots-Irish heading to Augusta in Georgia, were attacked by Cherokee warriors and 23 were killed. The Calhouns were among the families attacked and 76-year-old grandmother Catherine Montgomery Calhoun, her son James and grand-daughter Catherine were killed. Other children Ann and Mary were captured and taken away to be raised by Indian squaws. Ann was allowed to return to her family 14 years later after treaty negotiations. This attack and other raids in that year temporarily halted the flow of settlers to the Abbeville region.

The barbarity at Long Cane was a fall-out from the French/Indian War of the 1754-63 period. Cherokee Indians of the upper part of South Carolina became allies of the British forces and went north with them to fight the French in Canada. After the surrender of Quebec in 1759 these Indians returned back to their homes in Carolina and while passing through Virginia they came into conflict with Scots-Irish settlers after taking horses. This act enraged the settlers and they pursued the Indians, killing a dozen of them.

The Cherokees were in revengeful mood by the time they reached South Carolina and several outrages were committed. The white settlers retaliated and one incident led to another. Settler families were moved out to the Waxhaws region and to Augusta, Georgia. The Long Cane massacre came as some families were fleeing their homes.

It was from this environment that John Caldwell Calhoun came and the traumas his frontier family faced probably explain the hardline policies he was to pursue as a politician. In 1811 John C. Calhoun married his distant cousin Floride Bonneau Calhoun, whose family was of the wealthy planter stock of the South Carolina coastal region. The move into higher society circles considerably advanced Calhoun's career. He died in Washington, in 1850 aged 68, and is buried in St. Philip's churchyard in Charleston. Fort Hill in South Carolina (today in the town of Clemson) was the Calhoun homestead for the last 25 years of his life. The 1,100-acre plantation was acquired in 1825 and Calhoun named it Fort Hill, honouring Fort Rutledge which was built on the lands in 1776 as protection from a nearby settlement of Indians.

John C. and Floride Bonneau Calhoun had 10 children, seven of whom lived to adulthood. One of the daughters Anna Maria married noted American educationalist and artist Thomas Green Clemson, who was also in the diplomatic service as Charge d'affairs to Belgium. He became the first Superintendent of Agriculture for the United States in 1860, but resigned after a year on the outbreak of Civil War. The Clemsons lived at Fort Hill after John C. Calhoun passed on and they bequeathed the plantation and about 80,000 dollars to the state of South Carolina for the establishment of a scientific and agricultural college. Today Clemson University occupies the site.

* One of John C. Calhoun's overseers on his Abbeville estate was Patrick Cain, who left the north of Ireland for America as a young man, serving in the South Carolina Militia during the Revolutionary War. His 10-year-old son John was a drummer boy in the American Continental Army. Patrick's wife Susan Crawford was also of Ulster stock and the couple's family are believed to have emigrated as part of the movement organised in the early 1770s by the Rev. William Martin and his Covenanting associates.

The Pickens *of South Carolina*

Andrew Pickens was a distinguished soldier in South Carolina through the Revolutionary War period. He came of Protestant, Huguenot and Presbyterian stock, his parents Andrew and Nancy Davis Pickens had emigrated from the north of Ireland in the early 18th century. William Pickens and his wife Margaret, Andrew's grandparents, came to Pennsylvania from Ulster in 1720 with their six sons and in 1740 the family settled in Augusta County, Virginia when the Shenandoah lands were being opened up.

The Pickens family moved to South Carolina about 1750 and young Andrew married Rebecca Calhoun, a first cousin of John C. Calhoun, the leading South Carolina statesman and politician of the early 19th century and another son of a Scots-Irish family. The family lived for 10 years on 800 acres in the Waxhaws region along the borders of North and South Carolina and it was when they later moved to Abbeville that Andrew emerged as a leading citizen.

This tall, lean, austere man was a born leader. He was no speech-maker, but when he spoke everyone listened. His leadership against the Cherokee Indian assaults of the Carolina back-country settlements in 1776 advanced his reputation and by 1779 Pickens was a colonel commanding one of the foremost militia regiments in South Carolina. To the Cherokees, Pickens was known as Skyaguusta – "the wizard owl." The Cherokees feared and honoured him as a battle leader who had defeated them repeatedly on their home ground. Pickens was a believer in fair treatment for the Indian nations. He was convinced that whites and Indians could live harmoniously, each on their own lands, and believed the treaties he helped to frame were just to both races. He was deeply disappointed by the way the Indians were treated in later years.

Andrew Pickens took part in the fighting at Ninety Six and afterwards he helped to negotiate a treaty with the loyalists. He was essentially a farmer in the traditional frontiersman mould and a justice of the peace, but as a militia officer he was in the top category, rising to Brigadier General. After the fall of Charleston and Camden in 1780, Pickens was captured and paroled, but when British forces burned his house he broke the parole and rejoined the Revolutionaries. At the Battle of Cowpens in January 1781, Pickens rallied the militia to defeat the British and for this service the U.S. Congress awarded him a sword. His son Robert also fought at Cowpens, as a lieutenant.

Pickens was elected to the South Carolina state legislature in 1782 and in the same year he raised and commanded a company of 500 men, which in six weeks defeated the warring Cherokee tribes. He successfully negotiated an extensive land treaty with the Cherokees in 1785, a deal that was upheld by the U.S. Congress. He served in Congress in 1793-95 and Pickens township (population 1500) and county in South Carolina is named in his honour. Pickens lived until he was 78 and is buried at Clemson in South Carolina. His tombstone identifies him as "A Christian, Patriot and Soldier".

A grandson of Andrew Pickens, Francis Wilkinson Pickens, was a South Carolina attorney and member of the State House of Representatives in the mid-19th century. He was a Congressman, state senator for South Carolina and American minister to Russia in 1858-60. At the outbreak of the Civil War he was Governor of South Carolina and demanded the surrender of federal forts in Charleston harbour.

Migration to the Appalachians

Scots have come to North America both directly from Scotland and indirectly by way of other countries to which they first migrated.

The greatest number of Scots came in the 18th century from Ulster in Northern Ireland, which had been settled mainly by lowland Scots during the previous century. Some quarter of a million people left principally the ports of Newry, Belfast, Larne, Portrush, or Londonderry to arrive after a period of weeks or months at New York, Philadelphia, or Charleston.

Scottish Highlanders came to the New World in considerable numbers during the 18th century - some 50,000 or more. The first major wave (produced by economic changes in Scotland) came in 1749, peaked in the 1770s, and ebbed with the beginning of the American Revolution. The second wave began after the war and continued to swell through the 19th century.

The majority of Highlanders came from the shires of Argyll and Inverness. Among the first were the dispossessed tacksmen, the gentry managers for the chiefs, of Clan Campbell and left from Argyll. Many other Highlanders boarded vessels from the Western Isles, Thurso in the north of Scotland, and Stromness in the Orkneys. The Gaels, preferring apparently to live among those who shared their own language and traditions, migrated to three main settlements - New York, Nova Scotia, and North Carolina. Smaller groups formed in Georgia and the other colonies, but the settment in North Carolina, started in the 1730s, was the largest.

16

The Kings *of the wild frontier*

S uch were the conditions in Ireland during the 18th century that very few of the immigrants to the American frontier thought of ever returning to their homelands. Their faces were turned in one direction and this probably explains why they kept heading west.

The King family, descended from Richard King who reached America from Ireland in 1725, were a typical Scots-Irish clan who extended out – from Pennsylvania to New Jersey, North Carolina, Tennessee, Missouri and Texas. Richard, a clothier, was, according to reports, "short and thick, in temper and manner quick, sociable, religious and affectionate to tenderness". His first wife Mary Ann died in Philadelphia in 1728 after giving birth to a daughter and in 1735 he married Margaret Barclay.

Richard's brother Andrew, who emigrated at the same time, was a tax collector for the port of New York. He was killed in a duel. Another brother, Robert, emigrated from Ireland in 1728, settling in Lancaster County, Pennsylvania about 1735. He was also a collector of taxes. Two other brothers John and William lived in Lancaster County, Pennsylvania and Augusta County, Virginia. Richard became active in one of the oldest and most esteemed Presbyterian churches in America – the Old Tennent Church. One of the early ministers of Old Tennent was the Rev. William Tennent, an Ulster-born cleric whose father set up the "Log College" near Philadelphia, later to become Princeton.

Richard and Margaret King had 11 children and in 1756 when good land became available for settlement in North Carolina they headed with others down the Great Philadelphia Wagon Road. They stopped at Salisbury, Rowan County and Richard's first grant of land from Lord Granville consisted of 574 acres near Third Creek. Within a year he had purchased another 331 acres from an Alexander McCorkle for twenty nine pounds. The land was described as having on it "a great deal of forest, but also a house, out-buildings, orchard, garden, pasture and water". Little wonder families like the Kings never wanted to return across the ocean to Ireland.

The McCorkles, also of Scots-Irish stock, were very close to the Kings after being together for weeks in the trek along the Great Wagon Road. One of Alexander McCorkle's sons, Samuel Eusebius McCorkle, was educated at Princeton and became minister of Thyatire Presbyterian Church, where the Kings worshipped and was a final resting place for Richard in 1782 and Margaret in 1785.

Tragedy struck the King family shortly after their arrival in Salisbury. The French and Indian War claimed the life of Richard King Jun. when, on February 5, 1760, he was killed by Indians on the banks of Withrow Creek, aged 20. Robert, another son, married Mary Morrison, daughter of William Morrison, who had emigrated from Ulster with his father and brother in 1730 and is claimed to have been the first inhabitant of the region. An inscription on William Morrison's grave at Morrison Cemetery in Iredell County reads: "And as he was the first inhabitant of this county and possessor of this land, he requested that this grave on the left hand should not be opened".

The King lands extended out, with Robert's brother James and John also owning extensive plantations. Robert was very active in the Revolutionary movement and responsible for organising local committees for resistance against the British. With others, in 1775, he met to discuss the acquisition of gun powder, lead and flints and the punishment of persons involved in profiteering. They raised a force of 1,000 men to fight the British and their Indian allies.

Robert King was appointed as a Justice of the Peace and he served as captain with the militia which was victorious at the Battle of Kings Mountain in October 1780. His service in the War of Independence brought him bounty lands in Middle Tennessee and with his family moved to Sumner County in 1791. There they belonged to Shiloh Presbyterian Church, which was organised by Robert's son-in-law the

Rev. William McGee. One of Robert's sons Samuel married Anna Dixon, whose father was killed by Indians near his wooden cabin home, and he emerged as one of the leaders in the Cumberland Presbyterian Church movement of the early 1800s.

Samuel was deeply religious, a leader of men, and he was selected to help fill the critical shortage of ministers in the Cumberland area of Tennessee. The Rev. David Rice, the oldest Presbyterian minister in Kentucky, recommended Samuel as a minister even though he did not have, and could not possibly obtain, the educational and theological credentials required. The spiritual needs of the people, however, had to be met and in 1802, despite his educational shortcomings, Samuel was licensed as a probationer for the ministry. In the same year the Cumberland Presbytery was formed and in 1804 Samuel became a fully recognised church minister.

Samuel and his group were known as "revivalist ministers" because they preached at largely attended camp meetings. A very strong revivalist movement was sweeping the Appalachian states at the time, but conservative clerics were against the camp meetings and in 1805 the Synod of Kentucky dissolved the Cumberland Presbytery. For several years King and his fellow ministerial colleagues Finis Ewing, William McGee and Samuel McAdow, all of Ulster-Scots stock, maintained their witness among the people on the frontier settlements. In February, 1810 at Dickson County, Tennessee they decided reconciliation was not possible with their detractors in mainstream Presbyterianism and the Cumberland Presbytery was set up as an independent denomination. The log cabin in which they met is still in existence in what is now Montgomery Bell State Park.

The Cumberland Presbyterian Church grew rapidly in the region, extending into Kentucky, North Carolina and Virginia. The Rev. Samuel King, accompanied by one of his sons, the Rev. Robert D. King, carried the gospel to the far corners of the territory. Samuel and Robert were particularly zealous in their missionary work with the Indians. In 1906 there was a union between some Cumberland churches and congregations of the mainstream Presbyterian Church (USA), but a considerable segment of the breakaway denomination remained independent. Today, the Cumberland Presbyterian Church has about 100,000 members and almost 800 congregations, located mainly in the

Appalachian states with some branches in Indiana, Illinois, Michigan, Iowa, New Mexico, Arizona and California.

The Rev. Samuel King was described thus: "He was a plain, practical man, whose labors were extensively useful. He was beloved of all his brethren, many of whom acknowledge him as their spiritual father. Although he had not a diploma from some prominent college, he had the approval of God to his ministry". King was strongly opposed to even the moderate use of alcohol and refused to ask a blessing on any table which had whiskey on it.

Robert King, son of the original emigrant Richard, died in 1806 and is buried with his wife Mary Morrison, who died in 1824, in the Old Shiloh Church Cemetery in Sumner County, Middle Tennessee. The Rev. Samuel King was left 64 acres of land from his father's will. Robert King was extremely devout, strictly upholding the Sabbath. One of his grandsons recalled how he had been chastised by his grandfather for throwing a stone at a squirrel on Sunday.

The Rev. Samuel King ministered in Wilson, Bedford and Marshall Counties in Tennessee, before moving on with his family to Clay County, Missouri, in 1824. Missouri was admitted to the Union in 1821, and King devoted most of his efforts to the organisation of Cumberland churches and he also acted as missionary to the Choctaw and Chickasaw Indians. In his later years he assisted his son, Robert D. in the pastorship at Old Shiloh Church at Post Oak, Johnson County, Missouri. He died in 1842, aged 67.

Samuel King had three other sons – the Rev. Finis Ewing King, Judge Richard McGee King and William D. King. The Rev. Robert D. King, his eldest son, moved to Texas in 1859 taking on the ministry of Shiloh Cumberland Presbyterian Church in Ellis County on the death of his brother the Rev. Finis Ewing. Robert D. was then a man of 60, with a patriotic zeal and he ministered to Confederate troops in Texas before they marched to defend Galveston in 1861.

• Another family of Kings, who emigrated from Ulster in 1770, settled in the Raleigh, North Carolina region. Robert King Jun., fought at the Battle of Kings Mountain and later settled at Abbeville in South Carolina. He and his wife Tabitha had 23 children who branched out to become influential people in Carolina society.

17

Arthur Dobbs - *founding father of North Carolina*

The man who had the foresight and pivotal role in settling hundreds of Scots-Irish families on the western frontier of North Carolinas in the mid-18th century was eminent Co. Antrim landowner and Irish parliamentarian Arthur Dobbs. This wealthy aristocrat was born in Girvan, Ayrshire, Scotland in 1689 at the height of the Williamite Wars in Ireland, but he moved as an infant with his mother to reside at the family estate at Castle Dobbs near Carrickfergus in Co. Antrim, the locality where the parents of President Andrew Jackson lived before their emigration to America.

Dobbs took an interest in the American colonies only after he had established himself as a leading public figure in Ireland and a highly respected member of the British establishment. He was High Sheriff of Co. Antrim and Mayor and Member of Parliament for Carrickfergus, and was an extensive landlord, described as "improving, restless, energetic and ambitious". His private interests were astronomy, meteorology, botany and bee-keeping, and he became a strong advocate of free-trade for Ireland in the wider world.

With British Prime Minister Sir Robert Walpole and wealthy London merchants, Dobbs set out in 1730 to develop free trade with North America, fearing French expansion in the colonies, and links with the Hudson Bay Company were developed. By 1733, Dobbs had risen to become Engineer-in-chief and Surveyor-General for Ireland and was responsible for the erection of the new Irish Parliament House in Dublin and many elaborate Georgian-style public buildings in that city.

The Hudson Bay interest continued when Dobbs persuaded the Admiralty to mount an expedition to find the North-West Passage and in 1741 two ships set out from London, with the operation financed by Dobbs and his merchant friends. It was during his third term as Mayor of Carrickfergus that Dobbs, in association with British nobleman Henry McCulloh, secured large tracts of land in North Carolina and on the Ohio River. The attachment to North America began in earnest.

Dobbs purchased a part share in 400,000 acres of land in the present North Carolina counties of Mecklenburg County and Cabarrus in 1745 after the deal was recommended to him by a Co. Antrim associate Matthew Rowan, who was surveyor-general in North Carolina at the time. When Anne Dobbs, Arthur's wife, to whom he had been deeply attached, died, this created in him an even greater feeling of restlessness. He felt inspired to plant Ulster-Scots Presbyterian families on his new North Carolina lands and with Matthew Rowan as his point of contact the trans-Atlantic links were forged.

Dobbs, then approaching 60, wrote to Rowan indicating that he intended "to take a trip to Carolina and take over some families, and servants to settle them there and see the country". He was unfamiliar with life in North Carolina and did not even know the exact location of his holdings.

He inquired of Rowan: "Which kind of artificers or servants should I take with me as most wanted there, such as carpenters, smiths, masons, and coopers, and what number would be proper at first or could be accommodated with provisions and necessaries to form a settlement? What kind of goods, tools should I take over with them, for I think if I could take a trip and fix several it would induce many more to go from hence and help to increase that colony? Advise me, if I agree with any here who can transport themselves, upon what terms I should agree with each family, the number of acres, term rent or produce, that I may know how to conduct myself in any bargains I shall make?" Obviously the thoughts of a meticulous caring man!

At this period, many Scots-Irish settlers who had arrived in Pennsylvania during the first two waves of immigration were heading along the Great Wagon Road into new lands being opened up in the

Shenandoah Valley of Virginia and the Carolinas. Dobbs had sounded out families in Co. Antrim and adjoining counties about the movement to America and offered generous inducements to take up the land. He was encouraged by a communication received in 1750 from William Faris, an early settler in Dobbs's land near Cape Fear, Wilmington.

Faris wrote: "Your lands on Black River would be very fit for stock to raise a supply for your upper country when settled. I have two places not far from your lands, with tenants or shares with what we call Cowe Penns, in which cattle and hogs are easily raised under careful industrious people. The necessary tools of hoes, axes etc., are easily got here if you don't send them from London, with a few for a carpenter or blacksmith which are useful hands in a new settlement, with nails, hinges etc., and a few cooper's tools, course stripped blankets and coarse beds will be necessary, with any low-priced clothes or house furniture, viz. pots, pans, etc. I doubt not Captain Rowan has mentioned most of these things, possibly some might escape him."

Dobbs was encouraged to not only plant Ulster settlers on his lands, but French Huguenots, Moravians and Palatine Lutherans from Germany. His desire was to "civilise and make friendship with" indigenous peoples of Europe in the New World, and, although his settlement policy was one of self-interest, he saw the development as an effective way to stem French expansion in the American colonies.

The first Irish tenants for Dobbs' lands sailed in April, 1751 in a Dublin ship, believed chartered by Dobbs himself. They sailed with an accompanying letter from Dobbs which described the emigrants "as my tenants and their neighbours and friends." As Dobbs was recruiting Ulster families as tenants on his American lands, he was also lobbying strongly for the position of Governor of North Carolina.

His tone was strongly anti-French and in a circular letter to people of influence in London he said: "I have for many years made it my business to understand and trade and to advance the navigation of Britain and particularly of the American colonies and as I love an active life, whilst my health and strength continues, could wish to have it in my power to do good and to contribute to the wealth of Britain which I could use to have it in my power to do by putting the colonies upon making such improvements as would be beneficial to Britain and to extend and increase them so much as to take off many more of our manufacturers, and by properly instructing and civilising the natives and laying a foundation for their becoming Christian and using them kindly by giving them an equitable trade to make them our friends and alienate them from the French."

Dobbs was appointed Governor of North Carolina in January, 1753, but it was 18 months before he managed to reach America. The French/Indian War had begun and the British endured an early setback in the hostilities, being pushed out of the Ohio Valley. In June, 1754, the 65-year-old Arthur Dobbs sailed to America on the ship Garland with friends, relatives and prospective tenants on a journey which lasted 12 weeks. His son Edward and nephew Richard Spaight were among the voyagers.

Dobb's first address to the colonial legislature of North Carolina reinforced his trenchant views of the French: "Let us all behave like generous, brave men and true Christians and for a little while confine our appetites and luxuries and part with a reasonable part of our wealth to preserve the remainder and our happy constitution in church and State. This will show the Gallic Monarch, and his insatiable ministry, that we are not to be intimidated or bullied out of our rights, and that if we should insist upon his romantic scheme of surrounding, confirming and enslaving us, that we shall jointly and unanimously support our valuable religion, liberties and properties, with our lives and fortunes, and that whilst we behave like brave men and true Christians we are sure of the protection of God, and that we shall not only be happy in this world, but to endless ages."

Dobbs toured his lands in North Carolina upon arrival in the autumn of 1754 and into 1755. He wrote of 75 families who had settled on frontier land he owned: "They are a colony from Pennsylvania of what we call Scotch-Irish Presbyterians who with others in the neighbour tracts had settled together to have a teacher, a minister of their own opinion and choice." His associate, Matthew Rowan, observed: "In the year 1746 I was in the up-country that is now Anson, Orange and Rowan counties. There were not then 100 fighting men; there is now at least 3,000, for the most part Irish Protestants and Germans, and daily increasing."

Arthur Dobbs wrote glowingly back to England in 1755 of his colony's progress and of life in the Yadkin region: "Yadkin is a large, beautiful river where there is a ferry. It is nearly 300 yards over. At six miles distance I arrived at Salisbury, the county seat of Rowan. The town is but just laid out, the courthouse built, and seven or eight log houses erected."

During his first year in North Carolina, Dobbs and his tenants faced hostilities from the Catawba Indians and he erected Fort Dobbs to reinforce defences, with an Ulsterman, Captain Hugh Waddell in command of 46 officers and soldiers. Attacks on the fort continued for several years, before the settlers succeeded in quelling the Indian unrest. By 1758 Dobbs, his health in decline, had moved on to an estate at Brunswick, North Carolina and, in 1762 at the age of 73, he married 15-year-old Justina Davis, the daughter of an eminent colonial family in Brunswick. They wed in St. Philip's Church, Brunswick, but it was an uncomfortable marriage. Later that year Dobbs suffered a stroke which paralysed his lower limbs. He partially recovered, walking with the aid of a stick, but in 1765 he suffered another stroke just as he was preparing to return home to Carrickfergus.

The Assembly Council of South Carolina had tendered him its "unfeigned and grateful acknowledgement of his labors". He died a short time after the second stroke at his home at Castle Dobbs, Cape Fear, Brunswick and was buried in St. Philip's Episcopal Church, Brunswick. His young widow later re-married, becoming the first wife of Governor Abner Nash of North Carolina. The Castle Dobbs estate fell to Arthur's son Edward Brice Dobbs, who had served in North Carolina during the French/Indian Wars and was also a member of the Assembly. But he returned to Carrickfergus and Castle Dobbs was sold for £300 to Governor William Tyron, who changed the name to Bellfont.

The Arthur Dobbs era in North Carolina had ended, but the outstanding contribution this redoubtable Ulsterman made to early American frontier life is recalled in the annals of the state. Arthur Dobbs is recorded as being generous in his desire to do his best to promote the North Carolina colony. He was noted as a zealous servant of the Crown and a staunch Protestant, but he was also considered a man of liberal views for the period. He thoroughly disliked the French and frequently warned of their expansionist policies. His characteristics were impulsive, obstinate and self-opinionated. However, his one outstanding achievement was bringing North Carolina, from a frontier outpost, into the mainstream of American colonial affairs. Arthur Dobbs of Carrickfergus blazed a trail on the frontier! Richard Spaight, nephew of Arthur Dobbs, married into a leading North Carolina family and his son Richard Dobbs Spaight followed the family line as State Governor.

• Among the Co. Antrim families who followed Arthur Dobbs to North Carolina were the Dobbins, a significant name in Carrickfergus history. John, James and William Dobbin were sheriffs of Carrickfergus and a kinsman Alexander Dobbin resided in the Granville area of the Carolinas during Dobbs's time there. It is recorded that Alexander with John and James Dobbin were in Lancaster County, Pennsylvania between 1736 and 1749.

• Carrickfergus is today a thriving borough of some 50,000 inhabitants, situated on the northern shores of Belfast Lough. It was in Carrickfergus that the first Scottish Presbyterian churches were established during the early Ulster plantation years of the 17th century, and it was at Carrickfergus harbour that King William III arrived with his army in June, 1690 before moving to the Battle of the Boyne, where he secured the Protestant succession in Britain with a victory over the Roman Catholic monarch King James II.

18

Leading the way *on the frontier*

Rowan County in the Piedmont area of North Carolina was the launching pad for many Scots-Irish settlers of the late 18th century who had moved down the Great Philadelphia Wagon Road from the eastern coastal ports. Early frontiersman of English Quaker stock, Daniel Boone grew up on the Yadkin River at Salisbury in Rowan County and Scots-Irish associates from this region joined him with pick axes in hand on the epic trek along Wilderness Road to Kentucky in 1775. The Boones settled at Salisbury in 1751 when Daniel was 18.

Rowan County was established in March, 1753 to bring a semblance of order to a wooded wilderness which was rapidly filling up with immigrants heading down the Great Wagon Road from Pennsylvania and Virginia. The Scots-Irish were joined by a significant number of English and German settlers and for 23 years Salisbury, the county seat of Rowan, was the farthest region of the colonies. From this settlement, covering the entire north-western quarter of North Carolina, 26 counties in North Carolina and the state of Tennessee were formed.

The Scots-Irish settled for the most part on the western fork of the Yadkin River, while the Germans, often called the Pennsylvania Dutch, took up residence to the east. All were of the Calvinist tradition – the Scots-Irish Presbyterians and the Germans with their Lutheran and Reformed churches of the Palatinate tradition in Europe.

The huge flood of immigration into the Piedmont after 1745 opened up the Carolina interior and as North Carolina historian Dr. Hugh T. Lefler relates the population increased dramatically within several decades: "In 1727 there were only 30,000 whites and fewer than 6,000 negroes in the province. North Carolina was perhaps the most sparsely settled of all the English continental colonies".

By 1752 the population had reached 50,000. Ten years later the population estimate was 265,000 whites and 80,000 blacks and North Carolina had become the fourth most populous American colony, exceeded only by Virginia, Pennsylvania and Massachusetts.

In 1771 the estimated Scots-Irish population in the counties of Rowan, Orange, Mecklenburg and Tryon in North Carolina was in excess of 20,000. There were about 15,000 German settlers. It was recorded that the Scots-Irish were of one religion, Presbyterian, and when they came into western North Carolina from Pennsylvania it was the Philadelphia Synod that supplied most of the early ministers. The Rev. John Thomson was the first minister to preach in the region, beginning in 1751. Over the next two decades the record of Presbyterian activity is a gauge of Scots-Irish migration and settlement in Rowan County with the Rev. Hugh McAden the principal witness.

One of the Rowan County communities which requested a minister was Thyatira, called then "Ye Lower Meeting House". In January, 1753, two deeds for 12 acres each adjoining the land of James Cathey, were given to this congregation by John and Naomi Lynn. The name of the Lower Meeting House was then changed to Cathey's Meeting House. In 1764, two ministers, Elihu Spencer and Alexander McWhorter, were sent by the Philadelphia Synod to readjust the boundaries of the various Presbyterian congregations and the church name changed to Thyatira. The church for 25 years had no permanent pastor, but had to struggle along with visiting missionaries until Dr. Samuel Eusebius McCorkle was ordained in 1777.

Another Scots-Irish settlement in Rowan County grew up in the vicinity of Cleveland and this congregation, although not organised, heard the same itinerant pastors John Thomson and Hugh McAden. There was located here a meeting house, a graveyard and a congregation among the first of whom were Samuel Leckey, George Niblock and Thomas Dickey. Samuel Young, the first settler to arrive here, was instrumental in forming this church called Third Creek Church. The church was organised in 1792, and its first minister was Joseph Dickey Kilpatrick.

The graveyards of these original churches are of the oldest in the county. The graves of John and William Brandon at Thyatira date back to May, 1756. Other notables buried there are John and Jean Knox, the great-grandparents of John Knox Polk, President of the United States; Francis and Matthew Locke, early patriots; and Samuel E. McCorkle, the first pastor of Thyatira and the progenitor of the University of North Carolina.

By the 1730s, land had become scarce in Pennsylvania, and expensive, while in the Shenandoah Valley of Virginia and North Carolina it was cheap and in bountiful supply. The cost of a 50-acre farm at Lancaster County, Pennsylvania in 1732 was £7 10 shillings, while in the Granville district of North Carolina (the Piedmont) a farm could be purchased for five shillings, regardless of the acreage.

The Scots-Irish were the first to reach the lush bottom land of the Yadkin Valley and the foothills which led to the Waxhaws area and the Blue Ridge mountain region. Most put down roots which have remained permanent fixtures until the present day, others had a yearning to move on to the new states which were opening up – Tennessee and Kentucky – and they pushed the frontier west.

Although there were a few settlers in the Rowan area by 1745, the largest numbers began to arrived in 1749 and listed among the Scots-Irish contingent of that year were: James Carter, Edward Hughes, Thomas Gillespie, Thomas Bell, John Davidson, Adam Carruth, William Sherill, John Dunn, John Withrow and Morgan Bryan, whose daughter Rebecca married Daniel Boone. The Gillespie family were gunsmiths who were to supply rifles to the militia at the Battle of Kings Mountain in October, 1780 and the Davidsons were revolutionary soldiers of distinction in the 1780-81 campaigns. The McCorkles, from Londonderry, and the Caldwells from Co. Antrim, were other Ulster families who provided leadership in Rowan County.

Edward Hughes was the first trustee for Rowan County and its main township Salisbury and when the Governor of North Carolina Ulsterman Arthur Dobbs visited the region in 1755 he reported the existence of "a courthouse, jail and seven or eight log houses six miles from Trading Ford". Dobbs also mentioned that 75 Scots-Irish and 22 German and Swiss families had been settled on the Rowan lands for a period of seven or eight years from 1747-48.

The Dobbs Trading Fort at Rowan County, close by the present-day North Carolina town of Statesville, was under the command of Captain Hugh Waddell. He came from Ulster in 1754 and was immediately sent with a commission from the west to protect the frontier. He had a garrison of 46 men and although there were hostilities with the Cherokees and Catawba tribes, Waddell successfully negotiated peace treaties with the Indians. Waddell later owned land in Rowan County and became a North Carolina legislator. He was heavily involved in the French Indian War of 1754-63 and was a contemporary of Major Andrew Lewis, son of John Lewis, the first Ulster-Scots settler in the Shenandoah Valley of Virginia.

Threat of Indian attacks confronted the first Rowan settlers on a daily basis, from the Cherokee tribes, but hostilities petered out after the French and Indian Wars of the 1750s/1760s as the immigrants turned to building up their communities.

One of the leading citizens at the time in Salisbury was Judge Richard Henderson, of Scots-Irish stock. He had an urge for exploring and sponsored an expeditional trip with Daniel Boone into "Kentuck" (Kentucky). Later, in the winter of 1779-80 Henderson joined two Scots-Irish contemporaries Colonel John Donelson (Andrew Jackson's father-in-law) and James Robertson in the hazardous journey from the Holston River in East Tennessee to the point at the Cumberland River in Middle Tennessee which today forms the city of Nashville. The three established Fort Nashborough in April, 1780.

Salisbury and Rowan County was the gateway to the west and significantly in those turbulent year leading up to the Revolutionary War it became the main gunsmithing centre for the Carolina Piedmont, with Rowan-manufactured rifles an important tool of survival. At the Provincial Congress of the Colonies at Newbern in 1775 (the year before the Declaration of Independence was signed) six of Rowan County's eight representatives were of Scots-Irish lineage – General Griffith Rutherford, John Brevard, Samuel Young, Moses Winslow, William Sharpe and Matthew Locke. The Provincial Congress became in the years leading up to the Revolutionary War a body largely with a patriotic American zeal dedicated to independence.

Towards the end of the 18th century, the Scots-Irish people were a dominant force in those counties generally encompassing the Piedmont region of North Carolina: Iredell, Mecklenburg, Rowan, Stokes, Cabarrus, Guilford, Randolph, Montgomery, Moore and Anson. Their fighting exploits were to major in the conflict which erupted between the states in 1861-65, with North Carolina very much in the vanguard of the Confederate cause.

The Rev. Jethro Rumple, in his History of Rowan County, described the early settlers of Rowan as "peaceable, industrious and law-abiding men who had come to this land to make laws for themselves and their children." They set up their own county government and courts of justice. According to Rumple, Rowan Count was not settled by Cavaliers or Huguenots, or by the aristocracy of old-world society. "We have good reason to be proud of the early pioneers, from Ireland and Germany, others of English, Welsh and Scotch descent. They laid the foundations of their homes, they were men and women who had suffered for conscience sake, or fled from despotism to seek liberty and happiness unrestrained by the shackles of a worn-out civilisation."

• Rowan County was named after Matthew Rowan, the Co. Antrim-born surveyor general of North Carolina during the 1740s. He was president of the North Carolina Council in 1753-54.

• Scots-Irish Presbyterians came into neighbouring Guilford County, North Carolina under the shelter of a church formed company, The Nottingham Company, that had earlier performed the same functions for settlers in the Pennsylvania and Maryland settlements. The company negotiated with Lord Granville, or his agents, acquiring 30 warrants for land in North Carolina. These warrants were sold to church members interested in going to Carolina for settlement, and ensured that desirable land would be available when they arrived. After the settler arrived, Granville's surveyor would survey the tract for them. Seventeen of these grants were completed, all in what is now Guilford County. Completion of these grants was interrupted by Lord Granville's death in 1763, the last known grant was awarded in 1762. William Churton surveyed every one of these grants. He was Granville's surveyor, and surveyor general for the colony of North Carolina.

Anno 1776.] HENRY AND ROBERT JOY. [Numb. 4075.

The BELFAST NEWS-LETTER.

From FRIDAY AUGUST 23, to TUESDAY AUGUST 27, 1776.

AMERICA.

IN CONGRESS, JULY 4, 1776.

A DECLARATION *by the* REPRESENTATIVES *of the* UNITED STATES *of* AMERICA, *in* GENERAL CONGRESS *assembled.*

The Belfast News Letter page one of August 23-27, 1776 with the European scoop story that America had been declared independent. The full text of the July 4, 1776 declaration was printed in full.

Appalachian *vocabulary*

ahind — *prep., adv.,* behind

airish — *adj.,* chilly, cool

apurpose — *adv.,* on purpose

at oneself — *adj. phr.,* at one's best, in possession of one's powers

back — *v.,* to endorse a document, letter

backings — *n.,* weak liquor left after distillation of whiskey

backset — *n.,* setback, check, reverse

barefooted — *adj.,* undiluted

beal — *v.,* suppurate, fester

bealing — *n.,* an abscess/boil

biddable — *adj.,* obedient, docile

blade   – *n.,* leaf of corn plant

blue   – *adj.,* of milk, blinky, soured

bone idle   – *adj.,* incurably lazy

bray   – *v.,* to pound up medicine

cadgy   – *adj.,* lively, aroused

cap   – *n.,* green leaves at top of berry

check   – *n.,* snack, light meal

contrary   – *v.,* to oppose, vex, anger

creel   – *v.,* to twist, wrench, become leaned

Popular Hollywood film actor James Stewart, who died in July, 1997, aged 89, was a descendant of Scots-Irish Presbyterian emigrants from Co. Antrim who settled in Pennsylvania in the late 18th century. James - whose middle Christian name was Maitland from his family connection - was born in Indiana, in the foothills of the Allegheny Mountains of Pennsylvania. His grandfather and father ran a hardware shop in the town, and like his father James was educated at Princeton College. A man of great integrity, James was a strong Presbyterian.

Maghera, Co. Londondery-born Charles Thomson, who designed the Great Seal of the United States of America and was Perpetual Secretary to the Continental Congress of America.

The Great Seal of the United States of America as expanded from Charles Thomson's original design of 1782

James Knox Polk, mid-19th century President of the United States who was born at Mecklenburg County, North Carolina of Scots-Irish lineage.

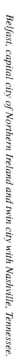

Belfast, capital city of Northern Ireland and twin city with Nashville, Tennessee.

'The Boy Soldier of the Waxhaws' - a young Andrew Jackson as an American partisan soldier during the War of Independence. Painting by Raphael Ganarosa.

Conestoga Wagon, built in the Waxhaws region of North Carolina about 1814 - used to transport goods to local and regional markets.

The Battle of Kings Mountain October 7, 1780, when a Scots-Irish dominated force of American patriots routed British troops. Picture by Robert Windsor Wilson.

Two Presbyterian churches which were founded by Ulster-Scots
settlers in the 18th century: above Thyatire Church at Salisbury in
Rowan County, North Carolina, and, below - the Old Tennent
Presbyterian Church at Tennent, New Jersey.

John C. Calhoun, second generation Ulsterman and Vice-President of the United States during the period 1825-32.

Arthur Dobbs, formerly High Sheriff of Co. Antrim and Mayor of Carrickfergus and Governor of North Carolina during the 1750s.

*Parlour in the home of early 19th century Scots-Irish statesman
John C. Calhoun at Clemson, South Carolina.*

*Master bedroom in the Clemson, South Carolina home of John C. Calhoun,
American Vice-President and son of a Donegal Presbyterian emigrant.*

The mill and general store at Newry, South Carolina founded by the Courtenay family who originally came from Newry, Co. Down.

FOR THE FLOURISHING CITIES OF

Philadelphia and New-York,

THE remarkable faſt ſailing Brig FRIEND-SHIP of NEWRY, burthen 200 Tons, with a New Medditerranean Paſs, WILLIAM FORREST Maſter; will be clear to ſail for the above Ports the firſt of May next.—She is roomy between the Decks, and as no more Paſſengers will be taken than can be comfortably accommodated, thoſe who wiſh to embrace ſo favourable an opportunity, are requeſted to apply immediately to Mr. George Woodhouſe, Portadown; Mr. Sam. Murphy, or Mr. John Carr, Rath-friland; the Owner Anthony Hill, Ship-wright, Warren-Point; or the Captain on Board.   And as the ſaid Brig is deſtined annually for the trade of carrying Paſſengers, it will be a further inducement for her Owner to do all that lies in his power to make the paſſage comfortable.

Newry, 20th March, 1792.

Advertisements such as this in the Belfast News Letter appeared regularly as Ulster shipowners tried to encourage emigration to America for profit.

Author Billy Kennedy inspects the historical marker of the birthplace of General Sam Houston (inset) at Timber Ridge, Lexington, Virginia.

The log-cabined Timber Ridge Presbyterian Church near Lexington (c. 1748) where Sam Houston's family were among the first worshippers along with other Ulster frontier settlers in the Shenandoah Valley from East Antrim.

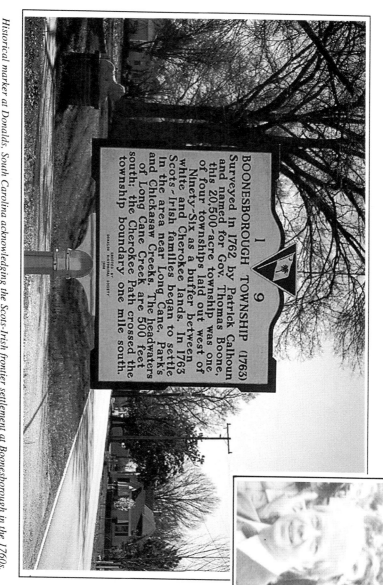

BOONESBOROUGH TOWNSHIP (1763)
Surveyed in 1762 by Patrick Calhoun and named for Gov. Thomas Boone, this 20,500-acre township was one of four townships laid out west of Ninety-Six as a buffer between white and Cherokee lands. In 1763 Scots-Irish families began to settle in the area near Long Cane, Park's and Chickasaw Creeks. "The headwaters of Long Cane Creek are 500 feet south; the Cherokee Path crossed the township boundary one mile south."

Historical marker at Donalds, South Carolina acknowledging the Scots-Irish frontier settlement at Boonesborough in the 1760s; Andrew Cowan, a forebear of President Jimmy Carter (inset), was one of the Boonesborough settlers.

Carrickfergus, Co. Antrim where North Carolina Governor of the 1750s Arthur Dobbs was Mayor before he moved to America.

*The old and the new: Knoxville founder James White's original log cabin shares the
scene in the East Tennessee city with modern high rise blocks. White, whose
grandfather came from Londonderry, first settled Knoxville in 1791.*

*Author Billy Kennedy book
signing on one of his visits to
Knoxville.*

The Rocky Creek, South Carolina site of the Covenanter meeting house of the Rev. William Martin, the Ballymoney, Co. Antrim pastor who witnessed strongly for his faith and ideals on the American frontier.

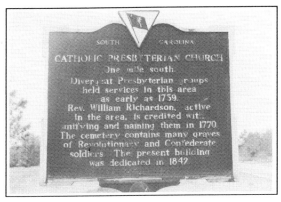

The site of Catholic Presbyterian Church in South Carolina, where Ulster-Scots settlers worshipped as early as 1759. Both Rev. William Richardson and Rev. William Martin were pastors here.

The tombstone of William Moffatt and his wife Barbara Chestnut in the Moffat-McDill-Strong Cemetery near Richburg, Chester County, South Carolina. William and Barbara sailed from Belfast to Charleston in 1772.

Memorial to Colonel John Carson, an Ulsterman from Co. Fermanagh and a pioneer of the Upper Catawba Valley in North Carolina. He was a representative to the Fayetteville Convention of 1789 in which the United States Consititution was ratified by North Carolina. He also served in the North Carolina House of Commons from 1805 to 1806.

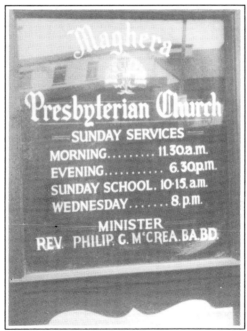

Maghera Presbyterian Church, Co. Londonderry where Charles Thomson, designer of the Great American Seal and Secretary to the first United States Continental Congress, was baptised. Charles Thomson's family emigrated to America when he was 10.

Author Billy Kennedy presents copies of his 'Scots-Irish in the Hills of Tennessee' and 'Scots-Irish in the Shenandoah Valley' to leading American country singer Crystal Gayle and her husband Bill Gatzimos. Crystal, from Kentucky, is of Scots-Irish extraction from the Blairs and Webbs in her family.

19

Sowing the seeds *of Independence*

The Mecklenburg Declaration of Independence drawn up in North Carolina on May 20, 1775 is widely acknowledged to be the preamble to the American Declaration of Independence of July 4, 1776 and Scots-Irish settlers were its instigators. This marker for the ending of British rule on American soil was ratified in a series of resolutions signed by the residents of Mecklenburg County on May 20, 1775 which called for the nullification of the authority of all Crown officials.

Mecklenburg, with the principal town Charlotte, was a hotbed of support for the American revolutionary cause, and because of the ferocity in battle of its militia, described by the British commander of the day, Lord Charles Cornwallis as "the hornet's nest". It was a region settled primarily by Scots-Irish Presbyterians and their influence was very pronounced in articulating the case for independence.

Colonel Abraham Alexander and Colonel Thomas Polk, as representative of Mecklenburg County to the North Carolina assembly, led the debate for the Declaration. Both were of first generation Ulster emigrant families, who had moved from the Londonderry/Donegal region in the first wave of emigration to America. Thomas Polk was a great uncle of James Knox Polk, United States President in 1845-49.

Abraham Alexander presided at the Mecklenburg Convention of May 20, 1775 and he was active throughout the Revolutionary War, both as a magistrate and a militia leader. Thomas Polk was joined in the fray by his younger brother, Ezekiel Polk, the grandfather of James Knox Polk, and, like Alexander, they were a thorn in the flesh of Lord Cornwallis and his Redcoat army.

Others of Scots-Irish vintage who came to prominence at that historic time in Mecklenburg County were Colonel Adam Alexander, General Robert Irwin, John McKnitt Alexander, Hezekiah Alexander, Captain Zaccheus Wilson, Richard Barry, John and James Flennikin, William Graham, Matthew McClure, Ezra Alexander, Henry Downs, Charles Alexander, Major John Davidson, Captain James Jack, the Rev. Francis Cummings, General George Graham and Colonel James Harris. Matthew McClure was Ulster-born.

Dr. Ephriam Brevard, the reputed author of the Mecklenburg Declaration, was of French Huguenot stock, whose grandfather emigrated from the north of Ireland with a family of McKnitts. Welshman David Reese was another with Ulster connections. His Welsh-born father David was a Presbyterian minister who was at the Siege of Londonderry in 1688-89 and later returned to Wales. Young David emigrated from Wales as a 15-year-old and married Susan Polk, a near relative of Thomas and Ezekiel Polk. He was a magistrate and a county court judge and was a main purchaser of firearms for the Mecklenburg militia.

At least eight of the 56 signatories of the American Declaration of Independence were of the Scots-Irish tradition. The Declaration, signed in Philadelphia on July 4, 1776, was a statement which enshrined much of the independent and democratic spirit that had been brought to America by the Presbyterian settlers from Ulster.

Thomas Jefferson from Virginia drafted the Declaration and the task of transcribing the document went to Charles Thomson, a native of Maghera in Co. Londonderry. Thomson held the high rank of Perpetual Secretary to the Continental Congress in America, the legislature which was then the alternative ruling body to the Crown, and he designed the original Great Seal of America.

Of the eight Scots-Irish signators, John Hancock from Massachusetts is undoubtedly the best known. He was the President of Congress and his signature on the Declaration was not only the first but the largest. It was reputed that King George III had bad eyesight and Hancock wrote large to make sure his name was not missed. On completing his signature, Hancock of Banbridge, Co. Down extraction, said: "There, I guess King George will be able to read that".

The other seven known Scots-Irishmen who signed the famous document were:

- **William Whipple** – his parents had arrived in Maine from Ireland in 1730.
- **Robert Paine** – his grandfather came from Dungannon, Co. Tyrone.
- **Thomas McKean** – his father came from Ballymoney, Co. Antrim.
- **Thomas Nelson** – his grandfather came from Strabane, Co. Tyrone.
- **Matthew Thornton** – from Londonderry, he settled in New Hampshire in 1718.
- **George Taylor** – the son of an Ulster Presbyterian minister.
- **Edward Rutledge** – another son of an Ulster Presbyterian family.

After being transcribed, debated and signed by the Continental Congress, the Declaration was then passed to another native-born Ulsterman for printing. John Dunlap had moved from a printing company in Strabane, Co. Tyrone to work in America in the mid-18th century and it fell on him the honour of printing the first copies of the Declaration. Later in 1784, Dunlap had the distinction of printing America's first daily newspaper, The Pennsylvania Packet. Soon after it was signed the Declaration was widely distributed throughout America, with the first public reading being enacted by Colonel John Nixon, whose father was also Ulster-born.

The first newspaper to publish the full text of the Declaration outside America was the Belfast News Letter, today Northern Ireland's leading morning newspaper and of which the author of this book is assistant editor. Details of the Declaration had arrived by ship frcm America in the port of Londonderry about six weeks after it was signed and it was taken the 100 miles to the offices of the Belfast News Letter, then published by brothers Henry and Robert Joy.

The news caused much stir in Belfast and for the News Letter, which carries the distinction today of being the oldest newspaper in the English-speaking world, founded in 1737, it was a European scoop. King George III in London had not even been acquainted of the news.

Massacre which *revulsed the settlers*

Buford's massacre at the Waxhaw region of North Carolina on May 29, 1780 was the defining moment for many Ulster-Scots settlers in the region who until then had not taken sides in the Revolutionary War. A patriot force retreating back to Virginia, the 11th Virginia Regiment, led by Colonel Abraham Buford was caught by Colonel Banastre Tarleton's British cavalrymen and nearly obliterated. So savage and merciless was the attack that Tarleton was despised as "a butcher" by the frontier settlers and it led many of them to enrol in militia units that were soon to see action at the Battles of Kings Mountain and Cowpens.

The wounded in Colonel Buford's force were treated in Waxhaw Presbyterian Church, by, among others, Elizabeth Jackson and her sons Robert and Andrew, later to become United States President. Robert and Andrew helped their mother stanch the blood on an improvised straw floor.

An uncle of the Jacksons, Robert Crawford was a major in the militia and the boys later witnessed the retreat of General Horatio Gates and his men up the road towards Charlotte after Cornwallis's victory at Camden. The Jackson brothers, both in their teens, were among 40 local militiamen assembled at Waxhaw Presbyterian Church on April 9, 1781 when a company of British dragoons attacked with sabers drawn. Eleven of the 40 were captured and the church set on fire. Andrew was detained for a while and his brother Robert later died from injuries received.

20

Harshness of life *on the frontier*

Most of the pioneering settlers on the American frontier of the Carolinas in the mid-18th century worked subsistence-type farms that produced barely enough to feed one family. These settlers enjoyed good crops when the weather was favourable, but they went hungry when frost, drought, flood and hail struck.

The houses of many of the early settlers, Scots-Irish and Germans, in the Piedmont of South Carolina and Western North Carolina were one or two-room log cabins with dirt floors and wood shutters for windows. It was common for the settlers to barter wheat for salt, bushel for bushel, and from the little money they acquired to buy sugar, coffee and tea or requirements for their holdings like a gun, an axe, a spinning wheel and iron pots.

Wages were low, with two shillings a day standard wages in 1762 for killing hogs, threshing and carpentering. Mowing grain paid a little more. One day's labour would purchase about one bushel of corn, half bushel of wheat, half bushel of dried beans, half pound of sugar, half pound of coffee, fifth pound of tea, one pound of wool or one pound of nails.

The possessions of the small farming and labouring settlers were few. Furniture was made by hand – a few stools, a table, shelves and a chest or cupboard of sorts containing the usual cooking utensils of the day. Beds were mattresses made with leaves or straw. Cornbread, pork, vegetables and fruit were the basic foods and the horse and cow were proud possessions. Chickens and hogs, of the "razor back" or "wind splitter" species, were also kept. The animals were branded and turned loose to fend for themselves most of the year, and were generally poor and scrawny.

Farming tools were made by hand and clothing came from deerskin and homespun, hand-woven cloth. Adults and their older children worked from dawn to dusk to eke out a living in the harsh conditions. Illnesses were treated with herbs and home remedies, with mortality rates high and life spans usually short. Prosperity did exist amongst the settlements of the North West Carolina frontier, but whether it was at the level claimed by North Carolina Governor Arthur Dobbs is open to question. Dobbs said that at the time of the French Indian War of 1754-63 that few poor persons dared take up lands in the west and only rich planters from the north moved into the Carolina back-country. Quakers were generally of a prosperous background and many of the Scots-Irish settlers who had held land for 20 to 30 years in Pennsylvania and Maryland had money and influence. The tradition was that tax collectors, justices and elders in the various Presbyterian congregations were men of substance.

Many of the early settlers could not read nor write, although it was generally accepted that the Scots-Irish were the best educated of the immigrant groups. Presbyterians usually had a school erected alongside their churches and their level of literacy was high for the period on the frontier. An indication of the high literacy of the early Scots-Irish frontier settlers is contained in a petition addressed to the Governor of New England in 1718 by 309 Ulster citizens keen to emigrate to America. Among the petitioners were John Caldwell, Alexander Richey and William Park, from Londonderry and it said that of the 309 names on the petition, there were only 13 who did not write their signatures. A high percentage of literacy indeed for any period in history.

Opportunities to socialise on the frontier were few. Men went to sessions of the county court and to militia musters, where drinking, gambling, wrestling, horse racing and cock fighting were common. Women, domesticated and committed to the home, enjoyed quiltings and sewings. Weddings and funerals were well attended, and religious services were also guaranteed to draw a crowd, with itinerant preachers advertised to appear at someone's homestead or in "the grove by the spring". Choppings, threshings, corn-shuckings, house-raisings and barn-raisings were events not to miss.

There was very little mingling between the Scots-Irish and German families in areas like the Waxhaws and Rowan County. They occupied different sections of the same regions they settled and for decades toiled away almost oblivious to one another's existence. The culture gap was wide and language barrier formidable, with the German settlers passing their language down to their children and grandchildren.

The objective of most immigrants was to obtain land, and with the Scots-Irish the desire was not necessarily to own it. Colonial authorities in the Carolinas often complained about the Scots-Irish squatting on land that did not belong to them. This trait may be attributable to the traditional mixed farming of cropping, herding and hunting by the Ulster settlers which meant that when the land wore out, the restless families moved on to fresh pasture. Scarcity of money was also a major obstacle for many immigrants in purchasing land.

However, the Scots-Irish as a people managed by sheer persistence to establish a dominant influence on frontier society. The German settlers may have cornered the more fertile lands, but the Scots-Irish became the justices, politicians, mayors, teachers, clerks and registrars in the Carolina cities and townships, stamping real authority as first Americans – their culture becoming totally assimilated to the New World life.

The Scots-Irish have been described as clannish, contentious, hard to get along with, set in their ways. A prayer attributed to them from 18th century American frontier folklore ran: "Lord grant that I may always be right, for Thou knowest I am hard to turn". Their thrift was proverbial, it was said they "kept the commandments of God and everything else they could get their hands on".

Concern *back in Ulster*

In April 1773 the Londonderry Journal expressed alarm at the high rate of emigration, estimating that some 17,500 persons had gone to America from Ulster ports since 1771: "The great part of these emigrants paid their passage, which at 3 pounds 10 shillings each amounted to 60,725 pounds, most of them people employed in the linen manufacture, or farmers, and some of property which they turned into money and carried with them ... This removal is sensibly felt in this country.

"This prevalent humour of industrious Protestants withdrawing from this once flourishing corner of the kingdom, seems to be increasing: and it is thought the number will be considerably larger this year than ever.

"The North of Ireland has been occasionally used to emigration, for which the American settlements have been much beholden: - But till now, it was chiefly the very meanest of people who went off, mostly in the station of indented servants and such as had become obnoxious to their mother country, In short, it is computed from many concurrent circumstances, that the North of Ireland has in the last five or six years been drained of one fourth of its trading class, and the like proportion of the manufacturing people. Where the evil will end, remains only in the womb of time to determine."

21

Hardy breed *in the highlands*

The western highlands of North Carolina is a region thick with people of Scots-Irish lineage. These settlements came largely as a result of the Great Wagon Road from Philadelphia passing through this territory. The settlers had passed along the Shenandoah Valley of Virginia, some put down their roots there, while others moved into the more mountainous parts of North Carolina between Salem and Asheville.

Arthur Dobbs, the Ulster-born Governor of North Carolina between 1754 and 1765, encouraged many of his fellow countrymen into the region where land was cheap, the climate mild and Indian dangers not as pronounced. Almost all of these early Ulster emigrants to North Carolina were farmers and they adapted well to the mountain environment. Their blend of mixed farming combined corn, wheat, barley and bean crops and the herding of livestock, cattle and pigs. Some of the farming techniques were copied from Indian tribes, with whom the Scots-Irish got on reasonably well on this part of the frontier.

Presbyterian missionaries had an important role in the Carolina settlements, one of the most eminent being James Hall, whose parents left Ireland in 1730, settling in Pennsylvania where he was born. Hall was an army chaplain and captain of cavalry in the Revolutionary War and when hostilities ceased he devoted his life to missionary work on the frontier. Churchmen like Hall were few in this wooded mountainous wilderness and, although some Presbyterian churches prospered, others closed after a time because of the difficulties in finding qualified, educated pastors. This led many Presbyterian families to join the ranks of the Baptist and Methodist movements.

In the first 30 years of the Western North Carolina settlement almost half of the farm families in the region were Scots-Irish, as were more than half of the most prosperous landowners. Scots-Irish leaders of western highland society included **Felix Walker,** whose father emigrated from Londonderry in 1720 and who served three terms in the US House of Representatives; **David Vance,** one of the first men to settle west of the Blue Ridge Mountains and a member of the North Carolina House of Commons, founder of Buncombe County and grandfather of a North Carolina governor; **Robert Henry,** teacher, surveyor, lawyer, physician, historian and writer; **James Patton,** Londonderry-born early Asheville merchant, and his business partner **Andrew Erwin,** a member of the North Carolina House of Commons.

James Patton, a weaver, who set out from Co. Londonderry in 1783 and eventually became one of Asheville's leading citizens, prospered as a merchant and cattle drover, working the Great Wagon Road. On arrival in America, he put down his roots for six years as a casual labourer in Philadelphia and accumulated enough money and merchandise to set out for western North Carolina. During his life, he saw economic activity in the region dramatically expand from the dire poverty of the 1780s to a period of relative affluence in the 1830s.

In a letter to his children when he was 84, James Patton said he left Ulster because of increased rents and an overwhelming desire to escape "the oppression of haughty landlords". His immediate goal in Pennsylvania was to find work and save enough money to bring his family across. He was an agricultural labourer, clearing other people's land. He even returned to his former trade as a weaver for spells, but it was in trade with the increasing flow of immigrants of Scots-Irish, English Quaker and German-Dutch extraction that he prospered. Patton made his fortune taking cattle north from the Carolinas and as a merchant selling dry goods up and down the country.

Agriculture was the main occupation of the Carolina highland settlers of the late 18th century and the slash and burn technique adopted from the Indians suited the Scots-Irish farmers. Farming on uncleared land meant girdling and burning trees, utilising the natural fertility and cultivating among the trees or stumps by hoe. As the soil wore out, new ground was cultivated and the process began again. With their livestock and crops, the mixed farming of the Scots-Irish gave them a firm foothold in the Carolinas.

By the early 19th century a prosperous rural society had been developed in the western highlands of North Carolina, primarily by Scots-Irish descendants of 18th century immigrant parents and some English, German, Welsh and French families. It was a melting pot of diverse cultures, with the Scots-Irish a dominant strain. The western highlands had been a main hunting ground for the Cherokee Indians who had lived in the region for centuries and when the white settlers arrived there was a reasonable level of co-existence once the land boundaries and treaties were established.

Census returns for the small communities of the western highlands of North Carolina confirmed the percentage of families of Ulster origin as high as 40 per cent. These settlers were drawn from large concentrations of Scots-Irish who travelled along the Great Wagon Road through Virginia into the Carolina Piedmont and the Watauga settlement of East Tennessee. More than 60 per cent of resident landowners in Buncombe and Haywood Counties who owned more than 1,000 acres between 1788 and 1810 were Scots-Irish. The majority of justices of the peace were of the same ethnic origin.

Inter-marrying between the Scots-Irish and the Cherokee people was not uncommon and in later years, native Americans in this area were to carry names like Ross, McIntosh, Murphy and Walker. Some of the Cherokees moved to Tennessee, Oklahoma and Georgia, but a lot of them stayed. The Cherokees, with their own Sequoyah language, were most populous in the hilly regions of North Carolina, South Carolina, Tennessee, Georgia and Alabama at the opening up of the Appalachian frontier. They were called the "Mountaineers of the South", but went into decline as a nation from 1750, when an epidemic of smallpox destroyed half of their population.

In 1838 the tribe was deported, by the U.S. military, to Oklahoma and their chief at that time was John Ross, obviously linked in some way to the Scots-Irish. In 1906 the Cherokee tribal government was disbanded and they became U.S. citizens. Today, the last remaining Cherokee settlement is based north east of the Great Smoky Mountains National Park in Tennessee and North Carolina.

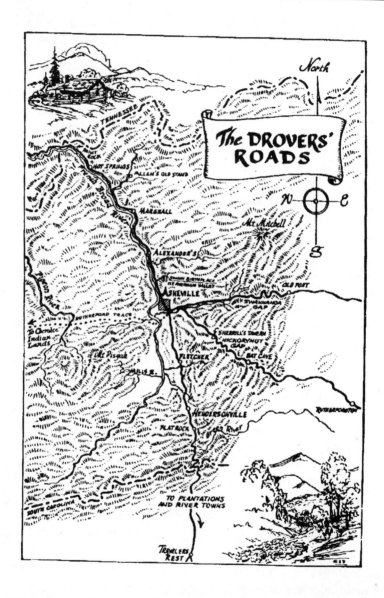

The Drovers' Road through southwestern North Carolina connected the region to Charleston and Savannah. It was a route of settlement in the early 19th century for many Scots-Irish families as well as the site of the cattle and swine drives that were so important to the regional economy.

22

Administering the law *on the frontier*

Legal authority on the American frontier in the mid-18th century was open to individual interpretation, depending on personal circumstances. Once townships were established, however, leading residents made it their business to have lawful courts set up on democratic principles that had their bedrock in Calvinism.

The first Rowan County, North Carolina court of pleas and quarter sessions, founded in 1753, was typical of a body administering justice on the western American frontier at the time. Justices appointed were leading citizens of Salisbury, the main town in Rowan County. They included a significant number from the Scots-Irish extraction – and the then youthful frontiersman of English roots Daniel Boone and his brother Squire, and Richard Henderson, who joined Colonel John Donelson, Andrew Jackson's father-in-law, and Colonel James Robertson, at the formation of Nashville, Tennessee in 1780.

Rowan County was the region settled by Carrickfergus, Co. Antrim nobleman Arthur Dobbs during his term as Governor of North Carolina, in conjunction with his Ulster-born colonial aide Matthew Rowan, the surveyor general of the state. The Rowan court met four times a year, with a lower magistrates court dealing with more trivial crimes and judicial matters, pertaining to tax assessments and land rights.

The court had jurisdiction in civil cases where the amount of litigation was more than 40 shillings and not in excess of 20 pounds and in criminal cases punishable by not more than 20 pounds in fines or imprisonment or corporal punishment. This court also had jurisdiction over legacies, estates, and orphans. The prosecutor was a deputy of the attorney general for the colony. Appeals could be taken to the Superior Court.

Apart from the legal duties, this court performed the functions of a government for the county. It submitted a list of three names from which the governor chose one for the all-important post of high sheriff, who collected the taxes – poll, county tax, and church tax for the Established Church (Episcopal). The sheriff also executed writs and summons, took charge of all properties held or sold by the county court, was custodian of the prison, inflicted corporal punishment ordered by the court, and attended executions or hangings.

The Court also levied taxes, ordered juries of men to lay down roads and build bridges, appointed road overseers, licenced taverns or ordinaries, and set prices to be charged at these. It licenced ferries and set prices to be charged at crossings and authorised the brands for farm animals.

During the colonial period the Rowan County Court licenced 142 ordinaries or hostelries (public houses) in Rowan County and Salisbury. The ordinaries provided meals and lodging usually in the operator's own home. In 1762 the licence cost one pound and ten shillings per year. Most of these taverns were unsuccessful. Only nine of the thirty tavern keepers in Salisbury remained in business more than one year, and only twelve in the county renewed their licences more than one term.

Tavern rates were set in 1755 as follows:
• Rum and whiskey and other spirituous liquors – six shillings per gallon.
• Dinner of roasted or boiled flesh – one shilling.
• Supper and breakfast each – six pence.
• Lodging per night in a good bed – two pence.
• Stablage, 24 hours with good hay or fodder – six pence.
• Pasturage, the first 24 hours – four pence.
• Every 24 hours after the first – two pence.
• Indian corn and other grain per quart – two pence.

The ferries which crossed the Yadkin, and Catawba Rivers in Rowan County were licenced and their rates set by the Rowan Court. These rates were:

- Wagon and team with four or six horses – five shillings.
- Cart with three or more horses – three pence.
- For every horse with a load thereon led – six pence.
- For every man and horse with saddle bags and other travelling furniture – six pence.
- Single horse, cow or steer – four pence.
- Footman – three pence.
- Sheep or hog – two pence.

Rowan County Court minutes of the mid-18th century recorded hundreds of actions concerning estates and orphans. There were no orphanages, and under the law the death of a father frequently put his children at the mercy of the court. The children were "bound out" as apprentices usually until aged 21. At certain ages, around 14, the child might choose a guardian, but this choice was not binding on the court. The apprentices were to be taught a specified trade and were to receive certain tools, clothing, and money, as ordered by the court.

Trades taught to apprentices in Rowan County then were: tinkerer, pewterer, cord-wainer, cooper, wheelright, turner and spinning-wheel maker, skindresser, tailor and shoemaker. Orphans were also taught to read and write and were given religious instruction, in the Reformed Protestant faith.

Rowan County may have been located in the wild frontier, but it had a civilised, structured society in the early years of its settlements, no doubt due to the God-fearing influence of the Scots-Irish Presbyterian settlers from Ulster.

Defending *the frontier*

The Dutch musket or bayonet was a favourite weapon of the Scots-Irish in the American War of Independence, particularly with the militia units in the Carolinas. But it was also used by the British colonists and frontier settlers a generation before in the French/Indian War.

Arthur Dobbs, the Governor of North Carolina and formerly first citizen of Carrickfergus in Co. Antrim, appealed in June, 1754 for arms from London that were "not of an assortment proper for His Majesty's Forces here". Within a month the warrant was issued in reply to the North Carolina request for 3,000 non-King's pattern arms and among them was a plentiful supply of the Dutch-Liege-style muskets with their distinctive bayonets.

The weapon was ideally suited for military engagement in the wooded mountainous terrain of the American frontier. The bayonet's characteristics were: a three-inch socket blade, mortise for bottom stud musket, a narrow flat blade with three flats on each face projecting from a raised oval guard, blade width 1¹/₈, blade guard from guard to tip 12³/₁₆, overall length 16¹/₄.

> *"It is against the law of God and nature that so much land should be idle while so many Christians wanted to work on it and raise their bread"* - the view of the Scots-Irish settlers of Watauga in North Carolina in the 1770s when facing British and Indian opposition to their annexation of land west of the Allegeny Mountains.

23

Native Americans *of the South East*

Throughout the 17th century the numerous Indian groups of the south eastern areas of the United States successfully held off their ancestral tribal lands against the establishment and gradual extension of empire by Spanish, French and English explorers. But a century later, with the European settlements on the American frontier, the Indian lands were seized or purchased in developments that were to signal the decline of the various tribes. The Iroquoian Tuscarora occupied the north eastern area of North Carolina. The Kautabus, a confederation of Siouan people, and the Waxhaws, one of the smaller coastal tribes living nearby, dominated the Carolina back country, the area now comprising the south central Piedmont region of North Carolina and the upper central reaches of South Carolina.

Other Indian tribes of the North Carolina region (about 1700 people) were the Coree, Wachapunga, Chowanoc, Pasquotank, and the Hatteras who occupied areas near the Atlantic; and the Cheraw, Keyauwee, Saponi, Tutelo, Occaneechi, and the Eno, who occupied inland areas west and south of the Tuscarora domain.

The Cherokees, of Iroquoian stock like the Tuscarora, held the lands along the southern Alleghenies from eastern Tennessee into the Carolinas and northern Alabama and Georgia. The Confederacy of the Creeks, the largest and most powerful groups of the south eastern Indians, occupied the areas of present-day Georgia and Alabama. The Yamasee people held the south eastern area of Georgia near the coast while the Yuchi held the area along the present-day boundary between Georgia and South Carolina. The Appalachee, Timucua and Calusa were established in present-day Florida, and westward along the Gulf Coast were the Mobile, the Biloxi and the Chitimacha.

The Shawnee held lands in present-day Kentucky. West of the territory of the Creek Confederacy lived the "far ranging, quarrelsome and aggressive" Chickasaw whose Chickasaw Trail to their land place on the big river (now Memphis) first led English traders to the Mississippi. South of the Chickasaw toward the Gulf, in the rich bottom lands of southern Mississippi and Alabama, was the nation of the Choctaw, described as close-mouthed farmers inclined to stay home and tend their gardens. They were bitter enemies of the Chickasaw.

Within the large territory extending southward from what is now the city of Charlotte, North Carolina, into the upper central reaches of South Carolina, and between the Rocky River on the east and the Catawba River on the west, lay the "Garden of the Waxhaws" and the historic Waxhaw settlement. The land lying between the two rivers was the hunting ground of the Waxhaw Indians. Wisacky, the village of the Waxhaws, lay south of the mouth of Sugaw Creek on the east side of the Catawba and along the banks of the Twelve Mile and Waxhaw Creeks. The Waxhaws were first discovered by John Lederer, German scholar and traveller, on the second of his three exploratory expeditions west and southwest from the Virginia settlements. Lederer and his lone companion, a Susquehanna Indian named Jackzetavon, arrived at the village of the Waxhaws on June 25, 1670. Lederer had left the falls of the James River near Richmond, Virginia on May 20, 1670, with a party led by Major William Harris consisting of 20 colonists on horseback and five Indians. The party pushed in a north-westerly direction along the course of the James River. When Lederer took a southward course across the James through present-day Buckingham County, Virginia, all members of the expedition turned back to the comfort and safety of their settlements, except Jackzetavon. Lederer and his faithful companion pursued their southward course until they came to the Indian trading ford on the Yadkin River near present-day Salisbury. After a journey of three days in a south-southwest direction from the trading ford, Lederer and Jackzetavon arrived at Wisacky. Westward, across the river lay

Ushery, the village of the Kadapaus (Catawbas) who were also known as the Usherees.

Geographically, the old and historically significant Waxhaw settlement included a portion of what is now Union County, North Carolina, and a portion of what is now Lancaster County, South Carolina. About 1740 the tribe of the Waxhaws were stricken with an epidemic of smallpox. The few who survived later joined the Catawbas and other neighbouring tribes, leaving the lands along the creeks uninhabited and unclaimed. It is thought the tribe was greatly reduced by the Yamasee War of 1715 and shortly thereafter united with the Catawbas. Land agents began advertising the desirability of this unclaimed, fertile and amply watered area but no white settlers entered the territory until May, 1751. The first settlement consisted of only a few families. They were joined by many others during the years that followed. Settlers had been pouring into the Waxhaw settlement for 17 years when Charlotte Town (Charlotte) was created on November 7, 1768.

The early settlers came primarily from two directions. Some migrated southward over the Great Wagon Road from Pennsylvania and entered into the land that was to be their home by way of the Trader's Path which stretched from Petersburg, Virginia to Augusta, Georgia. The Trader's Path, a route used by traders among the colonists of Virginia who pursued commerce with the Indians of the Carolinas and Georgia, passed through present-day Warrenton, Hillsboro, Asheboro, and came to the trading ford on the Yadkin River. John Lederer had helped to open this route for the fur traders.

A few miles from the trading ford was a popular camp site where travel-weary traders pitched their camps and rested. It was near this area, now Salisbury, that the Great Wagon Road from the north intersected the Trader's Path which carried families bound for the Waxhaw territory across the Yadkin. Passing near what is now Concord, North Carolina, the Trader's Path branched. The southern fork led southward through the Waxhaw country to Charleston, South Carolina, while the western fork passed near the site of present-day Charlotte and led to the tribes of the Catawbas and beyond to the Cherokees. In 1765 it was reported that more than 1,000 wagons passed through Salisbury a year.

In addition to the early settlers who moved southward over the Great Wagon Road there were others who moved northward from the low country. Many immigrants who landed at the port of Charles Town (Charleston) made their way to the well-advertised Waxhaw region to establish their homes and to find their destiny. Settlers in the area came from Pennsylvania, Virginia, the north of Ireland, England, Scotland, Wales and Germany.

At the "beginnings" of the Waxhaw settlement, the county of Mecklenburg had not been formed. The settlement was located in the vast Anson County, formed in 1748, which stretched north and south in a westerly thrust "to the South Seas" and covering areas now included in South Carolina. The county was named for Lord George Anson, a renowned English admiral and circumnavigator who had been dispatched to guard the Carolinas' coasts from pirates and Spanish raiders between 1723 and 1735.

The settlement of the Waxhaws lay in Anson County until December 11, 1762 when the Provincial Assembly drew a western boundary for Anson and made the territory west of it into the new county of Mecklenburg, officially established on February 1, 1763.

At the southern region of Mecklenburg was the Waxhaw settlements. Three counties were later taken from the originally large Mecklenburg – Tyron, in 1768; Cabarrus, in 1792; and Union, which included the North Carolina portion of the Waxhaw settlement in 1842. The area which is now Union County was until 1749 a part of Bladen County. From 1749 until 1763 it was included in the boundary of Anson County. From 1763 until Union County was established in 1842 one-half of the territory belonged to Anson and the other half to Mecklenburg.

The Old Waxhaw Church, organised by Ulster-Scots Presbyterians, was the first church to service the inhabitants of the area. It is now located in South Carolina, after being originally in North Carolina territory. The deed conveying the property to the church is recorded in Anson County, North Carolina, and stipulates property "Lying and being in the County of Anson and State of North Carolina."

The great Cherokee uprising in 1755 prompted Captain Andrew Pickens to organise a company of militia in the Waxhaws. Captain Pickens was married to a Scots-Irish kin, Rebecca Calhoun and was the father of General Andrew Pickens, the Revolutionary War hero.

24

Frontier community pioneers *at Watauga*

A merica's first free and independent frontier community, the Watauga Association – was founded in North Carolina in May, 1772 by settlers, notable among whom were a significant number of Scots-Irish. The first settlers of the Watauga and Nolichucky valleys were Virginians who had moved along the Shenandoah Valley from Pennsylvania. They were a hard-working, strong-willed, independent-minded people who, finding little semblance of law or order in the new lands they had moved to, decided to establish their own judicial, and civil system.

Five commissioners were appointed to decide all matters of controversy and to govern and direct for the common good of all the people. Two of the commissioners, cousins James and Charles Robertson, were of direct Scots-Irish descent. The others – John Carter, Zachariah Isbell and Jacob Brown – had English roots.

The Commission settled questions of debt, probated wills, recorded deeds, determined rights of property and issued marriage licences. It also had the ultimate power to hang horse thieves, who were then a scourge in the region. It was a form of authority which lasted six years and was considered by the vast majority of the Overmountain settlers to be an absolute necessity in a wilderness far removed from the law.

Lord Dunmore, the Governor of Virginia, blasted the Watauga development as "a dangerous example". He said: "It is an encouragement to the people of America of forming governments distinct from and independent of His Majesty's authority."

The Watauga community was in clear breach of British Government regulations regarding movement by white settlers to lands that were officially designated Cherokee country. Lord Dunmore reported back to London in 1774 that there were "a set of people in the back part of the colony, bordering on Cherokee country, who finding they could not obtain the land they fancied have set up a separate state". The Wataugans, however, were undeterred. They were isolated from mainstream authority, for outside the lawful jurisdiction of Virginia and geographically separated from the other settlements in North Carolina by forests and mountains.

Under the colonial laws of King George III they were squatters on Indian lands, but finding possession nine-tenths of the law they stubbornly stood their ground and ignored all edicts from Dunmore and the other colonial rulers. The Wataugans set up their own militia and entered into negotiations with the Indians, first to lease the lands from the Cherokees and then to make a permanent purchase. President Theodore Roosevelt, looking back 100 years later, described them as a people who "bid defiance to outsiders".

Tennessee's first permanent settler of record, Captain William Bean, arrived from Virginia in 1768 with his wife Lydia and established a home on the banks of the Watauga River, which was then part of North Carolina. Bean was an associate of the frontier explorer Daniel Boone, which may account for the Boone's Creek name of his Watauga home. Two years later, James Robertson, arrived after completing the long and arduous journey across the mountains. His stopping-off point was Sycamore Shoals (today in the north eastern corner of Tennessee close to Johnson City) and looking out over the lush Watauga countryside he was convinced that he had at last reached "the promised land".

Robertson was then only 28 and it was the beginning of an illustrious life on America's first western frontier which was to bring him honour as one of the founding fathers, not only of East Tennessee, but Middle Tennessee. With Colonel John Donelson, also of Ulster-Scots extraction, he helped found the city of Nashville.

Within a period of two years there were up to 100 farms settled on the banks of the Holston and Watauga Rivers and expansion along the upper reaches was rapid as more and more families poured in, very many of them of Scots-Irish roots. The west side of the Holston River was settled by John Carter (near the site of the present-day town of Rogersville) and it was to here that the grandparents of Davy Crockett moved. South east of Sycamore Shoals was the Nolichucky River, which flows westward from the Blue Ridge Mountains into the Tennessee-Holston Rivers. The first settlers there were John Ryan and Jacob Brown and both successfully traded with Cherokee tribes.

The Nolichucky settlement was not originally aligned with the Watauga Association, but as the Revolutionary War progressed they forged close links. The Cherokee Indians who lived in villages south of the Watauga settlements were understandably upset.

On one occasion the Indian concern was expressed to Governor Martin, of North Carolina by John Stuart, the superintendent of Indian Affairs: "The Cherokee Nation is still extremely uneasy at the encroachment of the white people on their hunting grounds at Watauga River, where a very large settlement is formed upwards of fifty miles beyond the established boundary, and, as I am apprehensive that it consists of emigrants from your Province to which it is contiguous, I must beg your excellency's interposition to endeavour to prevail on them to remove; otherwise, the serious consequences may in a little time prove very fatal . .. . should they then neglect to move off, I am much afraid it will be impossible to restrain the Indians from taking redress themselves by robbing and perhaps murdering some of them."

Despite the threats from Indians and official disapproval by agents of the British government, the Watauga settlers and their neighbours were resolutely determined to develop the area as their permanent home. For the first two years of the Association, the Wataugans lived in relative peace with their lease-holders the Cherokees, but the calm was broken by a few white settlers who still held grudges over earlier Indian attacks on their kinsfolk. An Indian was shot dead in 1774 while attending sports organised by the white settlers at Sycamore Shoals and, when all the tribesmen returned immediately to their camps, the situation became ominous. James Robertson, however, intervened and with a companion spoke directly to the Cherokee chiefs, expressing regret and offering to make amends for the terrible misdeed of a rogue settler. The Cherokees were pacified, but the war drums of the Shawnee tribes in the upper Ohio River region were beating loudly and hostilities continued through the Revolutionary War.

The cost of the Revolutionary War had left North Carolina virtually bankrupt and with thousands of her people now living west of the Alleghenies there was the problem of lifting land dues and taxes. Mountain settlers like the Wataugans were a fiercely independent breed, nurtured by the dominant Scots-Irish influences. They bluntly refused to heed any tariff directives from a state which had given them absolutely no military protection when they moved west, nor established any form of authority for them in the new lands.

After years of trying to bring the Overmountain people to heel, the North Carolina legislature in April, 1784 ceded the state's western lands to a Confederation Congress. Right away steps were taken to set in motion the embryo of a new state.

A series of meetings at Jonesborough, representative of the three western North Carolina counties – Washington, Sullivan and Greene, authorised the establishment of a new state of Franklin and its first General Assembly met in March, 1785. The state was named after American statesman Benjamin Franklin; the first governor was John Sevier, the hero of Kings Mountain and the secretary of state was Landon Carter, son of early Watauga pioneer, John Carter. Franklin was effectively the successor to the Watauga Association, with the Holston, Watauga and Nolichucky settlements all represented. North Carolina refused to recognise the new state and successfully blocked its application to the American Continental Congress. For several years confusion reigned with the people of the region facing demands from two state courts, two tax laws and two sets of state officials.

The rule of the new Franklin legislature gradually became untenable and by 1789 it had disappeared completely. George Washington had just become American President and, when North Carolina finally decided to cede its western lands, the region's affairs came under the control of the Continental Congress. This land was referred to as "The Territory of the United States of America South of the River Ohio". It included Kentucky county which was under the control of Virginia until 1792, when Kentucky became a state, and the region that today is Alabama and Mississippi. There was also the area which today roughly coincides with the boundaries of Tennessee.

25

Scots-Irish loyalists *in the*
American Revolution

BY DR. BOBBY GILMER MOSS

The foundation for creating a strong Scots-Irish force loyal to the King of England was laid four decades before the outbreak of hostilities in the American revolution. Beginning in the 1730s ten townships were created in an arc about 100 miles inland from Charleston, as a buffer against the Cherokee Indians.

To induce settlers to occupy this frontier, a series of acts were passed which resulted in giving free bounty land to any poor European Protestants. Of all the national groups which responded, English, German, Swiss and Ulster-Scot, it was the latter that came in the largest number, were most successful as frontiersmen, and contributed the greater number of individuals to the ranks of the loyalists when the Revolution began.

Ironically, it was the Ulster-Scots group that also supplied the largest number of soldiers to the patriot side during the war. Of the ten townships, Belfast (later often called Londonborough or Londonderry) lying on both sides of Hard Labor Creek above its junction with Cuffeetown Creek and Williamsburg (especially around "The King's Tree" on Black River) which drew the largest settlements of Scots-Irish Protestants.

Beginning shortly before 1760, the Ulster-Scots swarmed into the back-country. In 1759 the development of the back-country was interrupted by the Cherokee Indian War. From 1763, until the fifth year of the Revolution (1780), the migration of Scot-Irishmen into the South

Carolina frontier was annually greater than during any other period previously. It was also in this time period that large numbers of migrants from the North of Ireland began to arrive in Charleston, South Carolina, bound for the back-country.

Moses Kirkland, John Phillips, Joshua English, and Andrew Williamson, all having ties in the North of Ireland (though Williamson was a native of Scotland), greatly influenced the Ulster Scots who settled in areas around Stevens Creek, Hard Labor Creek, and eastward to Broad River. Kirkland and Williamson had arrived in the area early and by the 1750s had amassed large tracts of land. Phillips came to South Carolina in 1770. Kirkland owned a sawmill, ran a ferry, and held a large number of slaves to manage his industries and care for his large crops and cattle. Williamson was at first a cattle and hog driver for the militia posts near the Savannah River before he settled on his plantation, Whitehall, on Hard Labor Creek where he raised cattle and wheat. Phillips owned large tracts of land.

To the east of Belfast Township, the settlers in the area of "The King's Tree" in the valley of the Wateree River came under the influence of Joshua English, an Irish Quaker, who had settled at Pinetree Hill (later called Camden) in the 1750s. Between these two settlements of Scots-Irish lay Phillip's stronghold in the Broad River Valley from Winnsboro to the North Carolina line.

Alexander Chesney and those connected with him by kinship, settlement, and war experience, are typical of the average Scots-Irish loyalist. Chesney's experiences and activities, with a few exceptions, mirror the other Scots-Irish loyalists. He accurately represents all the Scots-Irish in South Carolina because he left behind the most detailed account of his experiences in the War of all Southern loyalists. His original diary is preserved in the Public Record Office in Belfast, Northern Ireland.

Alexander Chesney's kinsmen married into the families of Purdy, Gillespey, Archbold, Wilson, Symonton, Cook, Nisbet, Grier, Wylie, McCleland, Barclay, Pogue, Phillips, Brandon and others. By studying the Chesney family, one becomes acquainted with at least fifteen other Scots-Irish families which migrated to South Carolina and settled in the same area. By tracing the relationship of almost any other Ulster migrant family, one discovers a like number of Scots-Irishmen.

Alexander Chesney was born on September 16, 1756 at Dunclug near Ballymena in Co. Antrim. His father was Robert McChesney (note that the family dropped the "Mc") and his mother was Jane Fulton. On August 25, 1772, he, with his parents, his three brothers and four sisters, sailed from Larne aboard the James and Mary and arrived in Charleston about October 16, 1772. After a speedy voyage of seven weeks and three days, the Chesney family reached Charleston, but were not allowed to disembark immediately. Because smallpox was aboard the ship, the authorities ordered the ship and its passengers to ride at anchor far out in the bay for fifty-two days.

When everyone was declared clean of the dreaded disease, they were allowed to come ashore a few miles above Charleston. None were allowed in the city. However, this did not hinder the Chesney family because they already knew their destination. Earlier, kinsmen had reached the frontier of South Carolina and had sent written direction to their settlement site. In addition, the earlier settlers had temporarily claimed a nearby bounty land tract for Alexander and his family. Deeds to the land of many of these early settlers still exist in the South Carolina State Archives and they bear the word "Irish" written near the centre of each plat. The word "Irish" means that this piece of property had been set aside by the colonial government for settlement by none other than a Protestant Irish family.

Once ashore, Chesney and his father reached an agreement with John Miller, another Scots-Irishman to transport the mother and her younger children to the home of John Winn, at present-day Winnsboro, where they were to wait until Chesney and his father could travel further inland. The goal of the father and son was to find their relatives and secure assistance in moving the entire family with their small collection of keepsakes brought from Ulster. John Phillips, a kinsman by marriage, assented to fetch the Chesney family to his home site. He agreed to pay Winn one penny per pound for the use of his wagon to transport the family. In the Revolution, Winn, as a patriot, and Phillips, as a loyalist, served as colonels.

The Chesneys obtained 100 acres near the home of Phillips, cleared a spot, erected a small cabin, and began a farm. However, they received a letter from Sarah Cook, a widowed kinsman, entreating them to come and settle as her neighbour. The family dispatched

Alexander, their oldest son, to travel alone the sixty miles to the home of Mrs. Cook for the purpose of examining the situation and decide whether or not the family should abandon the labour they had invested or remain where they were.

Since the Chesneys did not own a horse and no road existed between them and the area in which Mrs. Cook resided, Alexander started walking through the uncharted wilderness in what he guessed to be the right direction for Grindal Shoals. Eventually, he reached the house of John Quinn, a blacksmith from Ulster, who directed him up the Broad River to the home of Ned Neil, another migrant from the North of Ireland. Here, he was loaned a canoe and directed up stream to the Pacolet River and instructed to paddle up Pacolet River a short distance, then turn to his right in Thickety Creek. There he found the home of Eliza Wells and was informed that he was within five miles of Mrs. Cook and other kinsmen.

With the aid of his cousins, the Cook family, and Charles Brandon, a cousin by marriage, Alexander found 350 acres of unclaimed land. Young Chesney hurried to Charleston, a distance of over two hundred miles, where he obtained title to the land in his father's name. He then returned to move the family further inland to Grindal Shoals. On May 26, 1773 the land was surveyed. This plot of land was bordered by John Grindall, Joab Mitchell, John Elliot, John Williams and some vacant land. All of the neighbours were Scots-Irish.

Only three exciting things happened to the Chesney family between the time their land was surveyed and the early part of 1775. The first and second events were the births of Thomas and Eliza into the family and the third was the shattering of the peace in the back-country. This occurred when the leaders of the rebels began an association in which all who signed the document refused to import or buy British goods and refused to sign an allegiance to the Crown.

Immediately, there was a serious disaffection to the Revolutionary movement in the back-country. The mere isolation of these regions prevented the frontier settlers feeling British wrongs as did coastal city dwellers or planters in constant contact with the restrictive policies. The most alarming resistance to the association was among the Scots-Irish between the Broad and Saluda Rivers who were exposed to the leadership of Phillips, Kirkland and Williamson.

To gain the support of these settlers, a programme was started to persuade the frontier settlers to sign the association. On July 23, 1775, the revolutionary council decided to send three men to carry out the mission. They were: William Henry Drayton, a Charlestonian who owned large tracts of iron ore rich land in the back-country and who employed large numbers of Scots-Irish and German frontiersmen as contract iron manufacturers; the Rev. William Tennent, a third generation emigrant from Ireland, Presbyterian minister, and a descendant of a famous Presbyterian divine, and a university graduate; and the Rev. Oliver Hart, a Baptist minister. The rebels judged that these three men were best qualified to persuade the Scots-Irish to join the war.

When the envoys reached Winnsboro, they met with the first group of Scots-Irishmen they had been sent to placate. They arrived late and found that John Phillips had the floor. Phillips, who was a recent arrival from Ireland, was highly respected by his fellow settlers. When he finished his speech, everyone except the two who had signed the association before he spoke, refused to endorse the association. Neither of the Council's agents were able to persuade any of the assembly to sign the association. These Ulstermen, many of whom had recently arrived in America, were enjoying unprecedented freedom and substantial economic independence compared to what they had lived under in Ireland.

Alexander Chesney and many of his neighbours chose to remain faithful to King George III, who they perceived to be a benevolent benefactor. In addition, their pride had been deeply wounded earlier by the disdain and contempt with which they were often treated by the coastal settlers.

In November, 1775, the back-country loyalists became engaged in their first military confrontation with the rebels. Although they won the battle at Ninety Six, they dispersed when they learned that a superior force was on its way from the coast. Chesney led many of the loyalists to the home of his father and secured them in caves along the river. From this time on many of these men served under Chesney and Col. Phillips. During the eight years of fighting, which included the important battles at Kings Mountain and Cowpens, they were found in the heat of the fray. Some of the Ulster-Scots who served with Chesney were: John Adams, William Atkins, Charles Brandon,

Christopher Brandon, Robert Chesney (the father), William Chesney (a brother), William Cunningham, Hugh Cook, Jonathan Frost, Matthew Gillespey, John Heron (a brother-in-law), Robert McWhorter, and James Miller. These and other Scots-Irishmen fought on the side of the Crown through the whole war. Some estimate that as many as 25,000 South Carolina loyalists, the majority of whom were Scots-Irish, at some time during the war bore arms against the rebels.

Though many of the Ulster-Scots were loyalists, it must be understood that the Scots-Irish fought on both sides. Sometimes father against son; brother against brother, and neighbour against neighbour were in battle. Ironically, some changed sides more than once as they conducted a bloody partisan civil war within the Revolution. The Scots-Irish were accustomed to fighting for their rights. Men on both sides had the blood of the defenders of Londonderry and Enniskillen in their veins. Such men were not easily cowed nor subdued.

When the war was over, some of the Scots-Irish evacuated with the British from Charleston in December, 1782. They went first to Florida or an island in the South Atlantic and from there to Nova Scotia. A small number left the cold North East and either returned to the South or went to England. A few, such as Chesney returned directly to Ireland, settling chiefly in Belfast, Larne, Ballymena or other lesser places in Ireland. There, they obtained minor posts with the British government, chiefly in customs.

The majority of the Scots-Irish loyalists did not evacuate with the British forces. Instead, they chose to remain in South Carolina and returned to their homes and land on the frontier. There, providing they had not committed barbarous war crimes against their fellow man, they were allowed to resume their place in society. Some were imprisoned, others burnt out, but a large number managed to mend fences with their neighbours. No one has yet been able to explain this phenomenon: men, who once had undertaken extreme measures in attempts to kill each other, once the war ended, lived together thereafter in close harmony.

• Dr. Bobby Gilmer Moss, of Blacksburg, South Carolina, is the author of 'The Patriots at Kings Mountain' and 'The Patriots at Cowpens'. He was professor of history at Limestone College, Gaffney, South Carolina.

26

Typical Ulster families *in the Carolinas*

THE ANDERSONS

Ulster-born William Anderson was a staunch American patriot who paid with his life at the end of the Revolutionary War in 1783. His brutal murder in Spartanburg County, allegedly by a band of Tories painted and disguised as Indians, shocked the frontier settlement in this part of South Carolina.

William Anderson was an elderly man at the time of his death. He had his head split open with a tomahawk and scalped. The attackers burnt the house of his son David, whose wife ran six miles to raise the alarm, with nothing but her night clothes on, wading two sections of the Tyger River. William had settled first in Pennsylvania and ran a mill at Connechocheague Creek. He moved to the Waxhaws, lived for a time in Charleston and settled in Spartanburg County in 1763.

Major David Anderson, the eldest of William's family of five, received a liberal English education in Pennsylvania before the family moved to South Carolina and he married Miriam (Maria) Mason, a member of a wealthy English family, in Charleston.

Major Anderson worked for some years before the Revolution surveying public lands for the Colonial government. When the war commenced, Anderson, fearing his house might be burned by the Tories or Indians, prepared a buckskin sack and sewed up his plat, surveys and claims against the government, and hid them in the hollow of a tree in the woods, where he thought they would be secure. At the end of the war he went to hunt for his buckskin, but found to his shock, the skin and papers were cut and torn into innumerable fragments lying at the foot of the tree, having been ate by squirrels. The labour of his years had been lost. Before the Revolution War, Major Anderson held a commission from King George III as magistrate. Espousing the Whig cause, he had a prominent role during the Revolution, participating in the siege of Ninety-Six, the battles of Eutaw Spring and Cane-brakes. He was a member of Captain John Barry's company, which marched in pursuit of loyalist leader "Bloody Bill" Cunningham after his raid to the up-country of South Carolina in November, 1781.

A grandson of Major David Anderson was General John C. Anderson, who fought on the Confederate side in the Civil War as adjutant of the 13th South Carolina Regiment. After the war he won promotion to brigadier-general of the South Carolina state troops and had a spell in the state legislature and as postmaster in Spartanburg. Another member of the family who distinguished himself as a Confederate soldier was Major Franklin Leland Anderson, who was involved with the Cashville Beat company, part of the 36th South Carolina militia.

THE BROWNLEES

Leading Confederate soldier in South Carolina, Captain John E. Brownlee, was the third generation descendant of Ulsterman James Brownlee who emigrated in 1768, arriving in Charlestown from Belfast on board the sailing ship Brigantine Lord Dungannon. The Brownlees settled at Abbeville in the South Carolina back country and Captain John E.'s mother Rosa Pettigrew was a member of a family who had originally moved from Co. Tyrone. His father John was a prime mover in the separation of South Carolina from the Union at the outset of the war.

Captain Brownlee served in Company 1, 14th Regiment, McGowan's Brigade of Infantry, and after the war he remained an unrelenting advocate of the Confederate cause. He became a wealthy farmer and served on the Abbeville board of commissioners. He was prominently involved in the Masonic Order and a leader of the "Red

Shirts" in opposing the Union occupation force in the years after the war.

When General William T. Sherman's Union forces were moving through South Carolina burning homes, buildings and crops, Captain Brownlee's ancestral home at Brownlee Cross Roads near Abbeville was spared by a Union lieutenant. He noticed John Brownlee's Masonic regalia on the entrance hall rack which his wife had placed there, and the lieutenant, himself a Mason, ordered his troops to move on. Captain Brownlee is buried in the cemetery of Little Mountain Presbyterian Church near Abbeville, which his grandfather William Brownlee helped to build.

THE CALDWELLS

Captain John Caldwell and his wife Margaret Philips emigrated from Co. Londonderry in 1727 and, after settling in Pennsylvania for several years, they moved with other Ulster families to southern Virginia about 1733. They found fertile land near the Roanoke River and Captain Caldwell became the first Justice of the Peace in the region. He had an estate of 1,045 acres and died in Virginia in 1750.

Donegal-born Major William Caldwell, the eldest son of Captain John and Margaret Caldwell, married Rebecca Parks, a member of another Ulster family. James Caldwell, the youngest son, was known as "the fighting parson for his deeds in the Revolutionary War. Educated at Princeton College, he was pastor of the first Presbyterian Church at Elizabethton, New Jersey from 1760.

Both James and his wife Hannah Ogden met tragic deaths during the Revolutionary War. The story is told that Hannah was sitting on her porch with her baby in her arms when she was brutally killed by British sentinels. After this incident, James became obsessed with getting revenge for what he saw as "a dastardly act". In the battle at Springfield, New Jersey he shouted to his troops, "Give 'em Watts, boys!" as they used Watts hymn books for packing to load their guns. The incident was made famous in picture, song, and story. A monument was erected on the spot to commemorate his bravery and distinguished leadership. James Caldwell died in a battle at Elizabeth Point, New Jersey on November 24, 1781.

Jeanne Caldwell, another of the family, married Alexander Richey, further cementing the Ulster ties on the frontier. Both were born in Ireland and after a period in Pennsylvania, they settled in Amelia County, Virginia in the late 1730s. Caldwell and Richey families eventually made it to the Abbeville region of South Carolina.

Another group of Caldwells came to America from the Larne area of Co. Antrim. They were members of the Seceder Presbyterian congregation of the Rev. John Renwick and about 20 families moved in this migration about 1770. John Caldwell and his wife Jane Helen Peden settled with their family at Cannons Creek in the Newberry area of South Carolina. Two Seceder churches were founded at Kings Creek and Cannons Creek and they became the mother congregations of the Associate Reformed Presbyterians of the South.

The Caldwells, of Newberry, were active patriots in the Revolutionary War and Major John Caldwell was killed. His brothers James and William, both militia captains, were at the battle of Cowpens and James survived injuries to become sheriff of Newberry district.

Martha Caldwell, a sister of John, James and William, married Ulster-born Patrick Calhoun and was the mother of the leading South Carolina statesman and American Vice-President John C. Calhoun. It was said in Caldwell family circles that the Calhouns were "nice people, but 'never amounted to much'," whereas John C. "got all his brains from the Caldwells".

THE CATHEYS

This family moved from Co. Monaghan in Ireland about 1718 and settled in south western Pennsylvania. James Cathey is recorded in 1719 as owning land on the Delaware River in Cecil County, Maryland; by 1724 he resided in Chester County, Pennsylvania and in 1733 held 200 acres at Lancaster County, Pennsylvania. Five years later his son William owned 466 acres in the Beverly Manor of the Shenandoah Valley and by 1743 the Cathey Virginian land holdings (at Beverly Manor and Orange County) had reached 2,350 acres. James and George Cathey moved to Rowan County, North Carolina in 1749, settling west of the Yadkin River in the area known as the "Irish

Settlement". The Catheys were a typical Scots-Irish Presbyterian family, whose prosperity came about through sheer determination and hard work.

THE COPELANDS

Brothers Charles and William Coapling (Copeland) left Newry, Co. Down on October 27, 1772 on board the Brigantine Free Mason, one of the five ships commissioned that year by North Antrim Covenanting Presbyterian minister the Rev. William Martin. They arrived in Charleston and received land in Chester and York Counties in South Carolina. William Copeland, son of Charles, had distinguished service as captain in the Revolutionary War, engaging at the battles of Ninety Six and Kings Mountain. A John Copeland, born in Ireland in 1760, is also listed as being at Kings Mountain in the role of lieutenant and it is believed there may have been a family connection with William Copeland. John Copeland was the hero of numerous battles with the Cherokee Indians.

THE COCHRANS

Benjamin Cochran was a Scots-Irish emigrant who had a price on his head during the Revolutionary War and spent a year on the run in Georgia from his Mecklenburg County home in North Carolina. This Ulster-born Presbyterian had sailed from Londonderry on the ship Admiral Hawk in 1758, aged 20, and on arrival at Charlestown he was given 100 acres of land. He moved to North Carolina and became involved in the Regulator Movement in Mecklenburg County which was pledged to independence. He was one of the famed "Black Boys" and had a conspicious role in firing a wagonload of powder destined for British forces just before the Battle of Almance. This led to demands for his immediate arrest, but he was never caught.

Benjamin Cochran and his wife Hannah Newell moved to the Abbeville region of South Carolina in 1804 when he was 66 and she was 46. His reputation in the Revolutionary War remained long after him and with a family of 12 children, eight sons and four daughters, the Cochran clan blossomed in North and South Carolina.

THE CULBERTSONS

This Co. Antrim family provided more officers to the Revolutionary army than any other family settled along the American frontier. The Culbertsons of Ballygan near Ballymoney were of ancient Scottish ancestry, and had been in Ulster since the early 17th century. In 1730 three brothers – Alexander, Joseph and Samuel Culbertson, from near Ballymoney, emigrated to Lancaster County, Pennsylvania. They settled in Lurgan, Franklin County, and called their settlement "Culbertson's Row", after the home of their ancestors in Ulster.

During the mid-1750s the Culbertsons migrated down the Great Wagon Road to Abbeville in South Carolina and there the families of James, Joseph, Josiah and Samuel spread out. Josiah served as a major and Samuel as a lieutenant and captain at the Battles of Kings Mountain and Cowpens. Robert and Joseph Culbertson, also listed at Kings Mountain, were engaged in the various Indian Wars.

THE ERWINS

This family of millers emigrated from Belfast to America in 1848 and established a mill at Saluda River on the outskirts of Abbeville in South Carolina. Malcolm Erwin bought 600 acres of rich bottom land on both sides of the river and established a saw mill, a cotton gin, a blacksmith's shop, barns and a brick hogpen. His plantation was a focal point for trading with the towns of Abbeville, Anderson, Laurens and Greenville and business prospered. Erwin returned to Belfast after the Civil War and brought Margaret McMurty to South Carolina in 1868 as his bride. Both worshipped at the Honea Path Presbyterian Church.

THE HAMILTONS

The town of Abbeville in the South Carolina back country was built on land owned by Major Andrew Hamilton, the son of Archibald and Frances Calhoun Hamilton, of Augusta County, Virginia. His grandparents were Audley Harrison and Eleanor Adams Hamilton, whose estate was in Co. Tyrone, Ireland. Audley was a direct descendant of

Lord Claude Hamilton a son of Sir James Hamilton, the second Earl of Arran and regent of Scotland and guardian of Mary Queen of Scotts from 1543-1558. His descendant Major Andrew Hamilton married Jane McGarra and in 1765 they moved from Virginia to Abbeville to join his mother's kin, the Calhouns.

Major Hamilton was a close associate of General Andrew Pickens, who had moved from the Shenandoah at the same time, and together they served in the South Carolina state legislature, as elders of the Long Cane Presbyterian Church, and as commanding officers in the Revolutionary War.

The Hamiltons had three log cabin homes in Abbeville burned by Cherokee Indians and the fourth on the site of the town's municipal hall and courthouse stood until 1871 when fire was again the cause. During the Revolution Major Hamilton had a number of violent run-ins with British forces and was for a time captured and imprisoned on his own estate. He commanded militiamen at the Battle of Ninety Six and with General Pickens was successful in pushing the British and their Cherokee allies back off the frontier settlements. Major Hamilton lived until he was 95, his wife 86, and both are buried in the Long Cane Cemetery.

THE HANVEYS

This South Carolina family dates back to William Hanvey, who and his wife Sarah were of Co Down stock and emigrated with their daughter Jane to Charlestown in 1767. Records in South Carolina show that William and his family were among a group of "poor Irish Protestants", who arrived from Belfast on the ship Earl of Hillsborough. William received 250 acres of land at Boonesborough or Belfast township near Abbeville and as a farmer he prospered. He was a firm supporter of the Revolutionary cause and almost a century later his descendants actively raised the flag for the Confederacy.

THE HILLS

William Hill from Ballynure in East Co. Antrim was an Ulster immigrant to South Carolina who typified the pioneering spirit that was so much part of the American dream. William, with very little earthly possessions, landed at Charleston in the summer of 1822 as a 17-year-old and moved directly to Abbeville, a region heavily populated with families from the same part of Co. Antrim.

The obituary to William Hill in the Abbeville Press and Banner on January 20, 1886 said he had come to America "with nothing to commend except his youth, his high integrity, his indomitable will, and the unfaltering determination to earn an honoured position among the people with home he had cast his lot". Hill brought various letters of introduction to various important people in South Carolina, among them Major John Donnald, a revolutionary war hero who had himself emigrated from East Co. Antrim to settle in Donalds close to Abbeville. He married Anna Hamilton Donnald, and set up business with a merchant store.

At the outbreak of the second Seminole War in Florida in 1835, William Hill heeded the Government call for troops to fight the Indians and he saw active service as an orderly sergeant. After the War he became involved in the mercantile business and his success in this field gained him such wide public acclaim that he was recommended for election as the region's Probate Judge (or Ordinary as it was then known). He efficiently held this post for 16 years until 1869, a term which covered the turbulent years of the Civil War when South Carolina was in the main vanguard of the Confederacy.

William Hill belonged to upper Long Cane Presbyterian Church and to the Masonic Order. Like other immigrants of his period he did not enjoy educational advantages as a youth, but through the basic university of life he became a respected leader in his community.

THE HUNTERS

John Bainford Hunter, born in Belfast on January 31, 1803, left home as a sailor boy for America because his parents were unwilling for him to marry at the age of 16. After landing at Charleston, South Carolina in 1819 he settled at Blairville, York County in the Carolina up country and his first employment was as a clerk in a local store. At Yorkville Hunter studied medicine in his spare time and graduated as a doctor there in 1829, practising until 1852. In 1830, he married Mary Morrison Jackson and they settled in Bethel, York County.

In December, 1833 John B. Hunter returned to Belfast for his father and mother James and Mary Hunter and sisters, who emigrated at his expense. They spent the rest of their lives in the Carolinas. As a young man John B. Hunter was thrown from a horse and from a wound he had a leg amputated above the knee. Tragically his death in 1852 came about through a fall from a horse. John B. Hunter had nine children, four sons and five daughters, and one son James Blairs Hunter followed his father into medicine. The family were leading members of the Bethel Presbyterian Church in York County.

THE JONESES

John and Agnes Jones with their two sons James and John sailed from Belfast to Charleston, South Carolina on the ship Earl of Hillsborough in 1767. They settled in Abbeville, South Carolina and both James and John became Methodist ministers. Descendants of the family later moved to Georgia and Alabama. It is not clear if the Joneses were Methodists or Presbyterians when they arrived in America, but there is a long tradition of Wesleyan ministers in the family, most notable of whom was the Rev. Samuel Gamble Jones. He was sent by the Methodist Church to establish the creed in Georgia and Alabama.

THE KENNEDYS

The founding father of this notable Mecklenburg County, North Carolina family was Captain Joseph Kennedy, who left his native north of Ireland for America in 1733. The Kennedys, originally from the Galloway and Ayrshire region of Scotland and thence Co. Antrim, settled in Lancaster County, Pennsylvania, before moving to Moffett's Creek in old Augusta County, Virginia, now Rockingham County, in the early 1740s.

Joseph Kennedy built a large stone mill at Moffett's Creek and this was run by his son Andrew when he and other sons moved to Mecklenburg County, North Carolina about 1766. Dr. Joseph Kennedy Jun., Joseph's son, was the first resident physician in Mecklenburg County and he served on the committee which drew up the Mecklenburg Declaration of May 20, 1775 against British Rule.

Dr. Kennedy died in 1777 during service in the Revolutionary War and his son Samuel became a Presbyterian minister.

John Kennedy Jun., a grandson of Captain Joseph Kennedy, was one of Daniel Boone's "30 guns" who cut the road through the wilderness from Long Island in the upper Holston country, just south of the present line between Virginia and Tennessee, across the Cumberland Gap to Boonesborough in Kentucky. He assisted in the erection of the fort there and during the Revolutionary War captained a militia company. John Kennedy Sen., was one of the earliest settlers in Rowan County, North Carolina and moved to Kentucky about 1775. One of his sons Andrew was active in the Kentucky militia and rose to the position of major. He represented Madison County in the Kentucky legislature.

The Boonesborough settlement in Kentucky endured frequent Indian raids and in one of these in 1777 John Kennedy Jun. was injured. He married Mary Anderson, the grand-daughter of Colonel John Anderson, a distinguished Scots-Irish patriot of Augusta County, Virginia. John Kennedy Jun. was killed with a James Leeper at the Cumberland Gap on December 26, 1780 during an attack by Indian tribesmen. Joseph Kennedy was taken prisoner along with a brother of James Leeper.

General Thomas Kennedy was probably the most distinguished member of the 18th century family. He joined the patriot army at Burke County, North Carolina in 1775 and was appointed captain of the mounted artillery. He served at the battles of Wilmington, Ramour's Mill, Cane Creek and Kings Mountain. He was wounded and captured by the British, being held for six months.

Between tours in the army Thomas Kennedy came to Kentucky, bought land from the Henderson Company in 1776, and in 1779 was appointed and served as one of the first trustees of the town of Boonesborough. He entered large tracts of land on Silver Creek and the branches of Paint Lick Creek and built his station on Paint Lick Creek in 1780, after he had led his company at Kings Mountain. In 1781, while Thomas Kennedy was away, his fort was attacked and set on fire. The courage of his wife, Agnes Ross, in tackling the flames and successfully defending the fort besieged by Indians is part of frontier folklore.

It was said: "The Boonesborough settlements were planted by men of peculiar vigour and were supported by a very resolute people acting under a corporation which was in a position to exercise some choice in the character of their colonists. Only men of character and courage were permitted in the district." The district boasted a large group of men of fine character and great agility. Thomas Kennedy, energetic, resolute, and daring, a man of force and high ability, played a prominent part in the establishment of the state of Kentucky.

Kennedy was one of the first to be sent from Madison County in 1788, and again in 1791, to the Virginia legislature; Madison County sent him with Joseph Kennedy, Thomas Clay, Higgason Grubbs, and Charles Kavanagh on April 3, 1792 to the Convention called to frame a constitution for the state of Kentucky. The Governor and member of the first House of Representatives were elected by a committee of 40 chosen by the district. Thomas Kennedy was elected as the first state senator for Madison County; General Isaac Shelby was chosen as the first Governor and on June 1, 1792 Kentucky entered the Union. Thomas Kennedy died in 1836, aged 79.

THE KNOXES

This Presbyterian family of lowland Scots resided in the Ballymoney area of North Antrim from about 1750 after moving there from Scotland. Life was harsh on the Antrim hillsides for Scottish-born James and Elizabeth Craig Knox and their family and they did not need much persuasion to take up the land grant offer of the General Assembly of South Carolina.

They sailed on the Earl of Hillsborough from Belfast for Charleston in March, 1767 and during a difficult voyage Elizabeth gave birth and tragically had to bury the child at sea. On arrival in Charleston, the family was allocated 450 acres of land in Boonesborough township or Belfast township, Chester County, 100 miles into the Carolina up-country. The Knoxes were of Covenanting stock and had 12 children – six sons and six daughters.

During the Revolutionary War John, James, Robert and Samuel Knox, sons of James and Elizabeth, fought with the South Carolina Continental Line, and were at Charleston when the British attack came in May, 1780. They also fought at Kings Mountain. James Knox Jun., was killed a year later by loyalists avenging the defeat at Kings Mountain. A cousin Captain Hugh Knox, who had been born in

Ireland in 1755, led the militia in battles at Rocky Mountain, Hanging Rock, Congaree Fort, and Kings Mountain. In 1793 he became sheriff of Chester County. James Sen. was made a justice of the peace at the age of 70 in 1783, four years before he died.

When new lands opened up in Kentucky, members of the Knox clan moved there in 1788 with other families in a train of six wagons. They settled at Crab Orchard, Madison County, Kentucky until 1812, when another wagon train headed for Bedford County, Tennessee. Elizabeth Craig Knox, the family matriarch, was involved in the various movements and she lived until she was 103, dying in 1822.

THE McCLURKINS

This Covenanting family came from the Ballymena area of Co. Antrim and they sailed from Larne to Charleston on the ship Lord Dunluce in 1772. James McClurkin and his children settled mainly in Laurens and Chester counties of South Carolina and they were members of the Rocky Creek Presbyterian Church. Some of the Chester County McClurkins moved to Ohio and Illinois at the end of the 18th century and were successful in business and the church. The McClurkins from Laurens County were reported in North Alabama and West Tennessee in 1830 and they were slave-owning farmers. The Tennessee family spelt their name McClerkin.

One branch of the Alabama family went to Arkansas after the Civil War, another to Texas and several individuals made their name as academics. Other members of the Ballymena McClurkin family came to the United States by way of Pennsylvania. They spelt their name McClurkan and had a number of Presbyterian ministers in the ranks, one of whom helped establish Tevecca College in Nashville.

THE McGINLEYS

This family originated in Co. Donegal after moving there from Argyll and the first emigrant James McGinley purchased land at York County, Pennsylvania in 1739. The family moved on through the Valley of Virginia and a grandson of the original pioneer was Lieut. Colonel James McGinley, a noted Revolutionary War soldier and a first settler of Tennessee. James moved to Maryville in Blount County, Tennessee in 1793 and was a militia officer during the battles with the Indians in East Tennessee. He was a founder of the old New Providence Presbyterian Church where General Sam Houston and his family worshipped. His son William Dunwoody McGinley was a prominent attorney in Maryville.

THE MORRISONS

This pioneering Presbyterian family of the Carolinas can trace itself back to John Morrison, who emigrated from Londonderry about 1788-90 and settled in Chester County, South Carolina after arriving at Charleston. John Morrison was born at Ballyspallan near Ballykelly, Co. Londonderry, close to the homeland of renowned South Carolina Covenanting pastor the Rev. William Martin. With his wife Elizabeth he moved to 100 acres of land at Buncombe County in North Carolina about 1800. A kinsman, Archibald Morrison, very probably an uncle, had also taken up land at Buncombe after which he moved to Abbeville County, South Carolina.

The Morrisons who remained in Co. Londonderry and maintained contact with their relatives in the Carolinas, carrying on occupations as farmers and weavers. A letter to John Morrison from his brother Daniel, of Ballyspallan, dated June 10, 1796 provides an illuminating backgrounder to life in the north of Ireland at the time.

Daniel wrote: "Brother, I would embrace an opportunity of conveying you a few lines if possible informing you. We are all well and in good health at present, hoping this may find you and family in the same. It is now so long since we had any letter from you that I know not well what to write. There are well lick to be trouble through this kingdom, but mostly in the upper ccunties between the Protestants and Romans and may from time to time have been killed in battle with each other and great many executed by law. There is another set now appearing called United Irishmen. These are not yet properly understood with us what their desire is. Nearly 20 of them was put in Derry gaol some days ago. What the result of this thing will be, time only can tell. Markets is very high, particularly cloth and yarn. Coarse yarn has been and is three shillings and sixpence to four shillings and twopence and fine from two shillings and eight pence to three shillings and four pence. Cloth of both sorts is high in proportion. Underefined flax is 10 pence per pound, refined 12 pence per pound. This country is greatly altered since you left us. Every article exceedingly high. Your father and mother are indifferent will at present tho a good deal failed. They take it very unkind you write so little to them. They hearby send their love to your wife and children. Your brother and sister joins in love to you all. We have had no letters from your unkel this long time. Send us word how they are and remember us all to them. Your unkel Clark is well, but your aunt has lost the sight of one of her eyes. I send this letter with young Hugh Wilson, who has gone into America this summer with his family. You will perhaps see him after a little. He can tell you anything thats a wanting. We hope you will write to us as soon as possible and let us know your settlement in that country, both in regard of your temporal and spiritual estate. Remember me to David and Jenney. I have nothing more dear brother, but conclude with my love and remain ever loving brother till death".

A further letter written by Daniel Morrison from Ballyspallan on June 16, 1802 to his brother John at Fishing Creek, Chester County, South Carolina read:

"I would hereby embrace an opportunity of conveying you a few lines, informing you hearby that we are well at present and hope these may find you and family in the same. We received your letter some few weeks ago which is all we had from you this number of years, only we heard by others that you were alive. Your parents were much affected at your indifference. There might be much said about it but I forbear. Your father is dead a year past at May last of a paralatick stroke. He took it in a minnet on the tenth of March 1801 and died the 10th of May. He lost the power of his one side viz: his left, and spoke but little during that time. The loss of an indulgent parent and a tender husband hath been sensably felt in his familie. Your mother, since that time, is very indifferent in health and much so at present. We are still in the same place. There is no change in the familie any other way since you left us, only William who is married – he had two childer alive and one dead. I have five alive and three dead. The living are Margat, William, Esther, Rosanna, and John. I live still in Haskel's house. The Socicity is held with me and Mosses Willson some days about. We have had very extraordinary times for some years past, both of wars and famine. Of both you have heard I suppose or I would be more particular. The dearth continued for ten full years. Often meal, the first years, was so high as 9 shillings, potatoes 20.20; the second years it was at 7.7 when shipping from America turned it, it continued high till the new crop, which was remarkable good and brought it to its old price. Meal is now 2 shillings and potatoes from 4 pence to 6 pence per bushel. Cloth and yarn sold high since this war began or we could not have done so well, and sells well yet. Cloth sells now at from 1.8 to 2.8 and yarn at 3 shillings per yard, good warp yarn at 4 per single and 4.4. With corn very high, I have known some large corn sold at 13 guineas, the common sort from six to nine. I hear now some cheaper barley was so high as 3.2 pr stone; beef from 6 to 8 pr pound, butter 14 and 15, and eggs here sold in town at 6k a couple. From these prices of victuels you may suppose what way those that depended on the markets lived for the space of some years. But thanks to kind providence times are much better. Let Hugh Wilson know his father is dead. It is now near a year since, his mother is alive but very frail. His father's Bible will be sent him the first opportunity. His sister Matty is dead and Tom married again to Betty Glen of Tartnakelly. His unkel Robert is dead lately. Nanny McGuineas is dead some years past. Your unkel and aunt Clark are alive but very frail. Ommit no opportunity of writing if you go back and let us know how to direct. Your brothers and sisters hereby send their love to you and familie and all enquiring friends. Give my love to unkel and aunt. No more but remain your ever loving brother to death."

In another letter to John Morrison from Ballyspallan on September 17, 1803, his brother William and sister-in-law Nancy wrote:

"This comes with our love and duty to you to let you know that we are well at present, thanks be to God the Giver of all our mercies. May they be improve to this honour and glory. May we know that we are not our own but that we are bought with a price and may we be found with Christ in the day that he makes. I would heartily advise you and yours to take good notice of what is therein contained and forget not the Lord Jesus Christ who preserved you in youth and riper years both by sea and land. We have two children living and one dead, the eldest James, just five years old, and Mary about 20 months old, and I'm expects another. Five and six pence a score, and yarn and cloth sells purty well. Your mother and James and the two girls lives where you left them and James follows the weaving. Your mother is but very indifferent in her health, but for the most part keeps the foot to live in a new house of Mr. Davis and follows the weaving unless in harvest. Your uncle and aunt are well and Hugh is now living with them after being ten years a soldier. Give my love to your uncle and aunt and all the parts of that family and to Hugh Wilson and famely. His father and mother-in-law are yet alive and in good health. I will not enlarge but recommend the perusal of the following letter to you and your family. Read it over carefully and you will find many truths therein contained and study the practice of them. I add no more but remains your loving brother and sister till death".

John Morrison had earlier on August 21, 1803, received a communication from another kinsman David Martin, who had settled in South Carolina. This referred to a letter that Hugh Wilson received from his mother and a few lines from Daniel Morrison which give account of them being all well and likewise of Daniel intending to come to America if he can by any means, and James Wilson's brother coming into the same region. David Martin mentioned about a ship that came from Belfast to Charleston with "people from Newton in her".

John Morrison died at Buncombe County in 1834, aged 66 and he is buried in the Barnwell-Morrison Cemetery there. His wife Elizabeth survived him by 13 years. They had 11 children – six sons and five daughters – whose families spread across the Carolinas and into Georgia.

• **Buncombe County in North Carolina became Henderson County in 1837.**

THE PORTERS

Ulsterman Hugh Porter, who emigrated to South Carolina in the 1750s, was a noted Cherokee Indian fighter and Revolutionary soldier. He lived in the Abbeville district and enlisted with the light dragoon regiment. He was captured by the British in 1781, but his 17-year-old son Philip took his place in prison at (New Bern), North Carolina. Philip was also a Revolutionary soldier and saw action against the Cherokees.

THE REIDS

The Reid family landed in Philadelphia from Ulster in 1745 and after living for a time in Augusta County, Virginia, moved on to Rowan County, North Carolina to join other Presbyterian kinsfolk. They were among the first to take up lands at Long Cane Creek in South Carolina, with George Reid, a man of considerable influence as captain of the militia during the Revolutionary War. George fought at the siege of Savannah and the battles of Cowpens and Ninety Six, his sons Samuel and Joseph were lieutenants in the war.

THE RICHEYS/RITCHIES

Four brothers Alexander, Charles, Hugh and Samuel Richey left Co. Antrim in 1727, arriving at New Castle, Delaware and setting up home at Lancaster County, Pennsylvania. Members of the family made it to Abbeville in South Carolina after James Richey Sen., son of Alexander, came over the land trail to Ninety Six District and staked out claims. He and his two sons John and Robert Richey fought in the Revolutionary War in Virginia and were noted Indian fighters.

THE SEAWRIGHTS

This Londonderry family first reached South Carolina about 1730 and settled at Kingstree in the Williamsburg county. William Seawright and his wife Esther Thompson and family had arrived in Charleston with a band of Presbyterians led by the Rev. John Baxter. Other Seawrights landed in Pennsylvania and migrated into Virginia and then to South Carolina. The various sections of the family received land grants at Camden County and members distinguished themselves as doctors, ministers, teachers, builders and farmers. Brothers Andrew and Samuel Seawright arrived at Charleston with their families in a party of 50 and within a short time they had acquired 1,150 acres at Boonesborough township in the Long Cane area close to Abbeville. Andrew was killed in the Revolutionary War and two of his grandchildren froze to death hiding from (Tory) loyalists in the cane brakes.

THE SHERARDS

Merchant Alexander Sherard lived in Co. Antrim, about 18 miles from Belfast, his family originally being French Huguenot Protestants. With his wife Martha Wiley, Alexander emigrated to Charleston in 1790 and settled at Moffatsville, Anderson District, South Carolina, where he founded a post office and a mercantile business. The Sherards were staunch Presbyterians who established a church at Moffatsville.

THE SPEERS

William Speer, born near Strabane in Co Tyrone in 1747, was at most of the Revolutionary battles on South Carolina soil and was widely renowned as an Indian fighter. His descendants became highly influential in the social, political, economic and military life of South Carolina and Georgia.

After arriving in America in 1772 and settling in Pennsylvania, William Speer moved to the Long Cane settlement at Abbeville just as the Revolutionary War was getting into full flow. He received extensive land grants for his war service and became one of the first white settlers on the upper Savannah River. There he farmed, ran a grist mill, general store and post office on a plantation called Cherokee Heights. He and his family were active in the Rocky River Presbyterian Church. Descendants include Alexander Speer (1790-1856), the South Carolina State Comptroller; John A. Speer (1834-1879), a Georgia Senator, and Daniel N. Speer, Georgia State Treasurer.

THE WALLACES

Co. Tyrone couple James and Eleanor McCullough Wallace sailed with their nine children from Belfast to Charleston on the ship Lord Dungannon in 1768. The family moved to the South Carolina up-country, settling at Abbeville. James Wallace became an extensive plantation owner and he was a captain in the South Carolina militia during the Revolutionary War. His four sons also fought in the war. Joshua Wallace, a son, married Elizabeth Smith, daughter of George Thomas and Mary Elizabeth Smith, another Co. Tyrone family who settled at Abbeville.

Family splits *over Civil War*

The American Civil War of 1861-65 split families, turning father against son and brother against brother. This was particularly evident in the Scots-Irish community, who in some instances divided irrevocably between the Union and Confederate sides.

The position of Dr. George Junkin, principal of the Washington Lee College in Lexington is a classic case. Dr. Junkin, whose family moved from Ulster to America in the 18th century, had two sons-in-law as officers in the Confederate Army – Thomas Jonathan "Stonewall" Jackson who married Eleanor Junkin, and Colonel William Preston, whose wife was Margaret Junkin, considered the Poet Laureate of the South. Dr. Junkin, 12 years head at Washington Lee, resigned his position on April 18, 1861 over the flying of the Confederate flag at the College, and sentiments expressed in favour of secession from the Union by colleagues. He asserted: "The right of secession is a national wrong. It is the essence of all immorality, it neutralises the highest obligations." His stand came after the senators of Virginia proclaimed their oath null and void, owing no allegiance to the United States of America and it led to a growing restiveness among the students, some of whom called Junkin a "Pennsylvanian Abolitionist" and "Lincoln Junkin". Despite Dr. Junkin's protestations, the flag remained on top of the main college building on the instruction of the Washington Lee faculty.

*In Virginia and the Carolinas, North and South,
it is reliably estimated that 40 per cent of Confederate
soldiers were of Scots-Irish origin. North Carolina
suffered the highest casualties of the War –
Company 'B' of Jackson's Guards
from the Waxhaws had the biggest losses of
any Confederate unit, 80 killed or wounded at
Gettysburg. The Waxhaws was a Confederate
stronghold.*

American country singer **George Hamilton IV** was born
and raised in North Carolina, of a farming family with direct
Scots-Irish and Scottish roots. Georve IV, who sings regularly in Northern Ireland at concerts and church functions, was
born in 1937 in the church township of Matthews near
Winston-Salem. George IV is intensely proud of his Ulster-
Scots connections and his solid Christian upbringing in the
Moravian Church which he has faithfully
carried with him throughout his long professional career as
a singer and musician. George IV, not to undermine his
Christian commitment, chuckles when telling a story about
his forebears at harvest time. *"Like other God-fearing
farmers in the region, they measured part of their yield
in gallons"* - reference to the fact that moonshine (illicit
whiskey) may have been distilled on the farms, as was the
practice of many Scots-Irish settlers on the American frontier
down the years.

27

Presbyterianism *in the Carolina highlands*

The western highlands of North Carolina has been a settlement for Presbyterian Scots-Irish since the latter part of the 18th century, but because of the remoteness of the region, churches have not been as strong as in other parts of the American frontier. The Concord Presbytery was founded on Christmas Eve, 1795 with twelve ministers and six elders. However, the first churches established in this part of the Carolinas was Thyatira or Fourth Creek (now First Statesville), in 1753. The original members were settlers who had moved directly from the north of Ireland or Scotland.

In the Valley of Pigeon River, at Sonoma (today called Bethel) Elijah Deaver erected a church to be used by any preacher who passed through this wild and desolate area. Sometimes it was a Presbyterian, sometimes Methodist and occasionally an Episcopalian. It is recalled that Episcopalian clerics caused quite a stir by wearing robes – an odd practice in the remote mountain country where people looked on this garb as suitable only for bed wear.

A number of Presbyteries emerged in western north Carolina from Concord, including Kings Mountain and Winston-Salem Presbyteries. Today there are close on 200 Presbyterian churches in the region.

A central figure in Presbyterian church life in the mountains of North Carolina was missionary James Hall, who first preached in the region in 1790. At the time three churches existed in the Asheville area of Buncombe County: the Reems Creek, Swannanoa and Head of the French Broad River congregations. An academy was established by

Scots-Irish Presbyterians of Buncombe County on land owned by William Forster (born, Ulster 1748). Robert Henry, a veteran of the Battle of Kings Mountain of Scots-Irish descent, taught in this the first North Carolina school west of the Blue Ridge.

The Presbyterian church experienced great difficulties in maintaining its witness on the Carolina frontier in the period of the Great Revival in the early 19th century. Many Presbyterians converted over to the Baptist and Methodist creeds. On a tour of the region, the Rev. James Hall reported that the state of religion was not as in years past. He denounced the "wild and delusive fanaticism" and the "horrid and extravagant conduct" in the services. Lack of qualified ministers was a problem.

Hall observed: "Our vacant churches in these counties still look up to us for public instruction and the administrations of the sealing ordinances of the gospel, but lament that they have from us too few supplies. From principles of necessity they employ preachers of other denominations to impart to them, some of their ministerial labours. For this and other causes, our numbers are dropping off, and our societies annually melting away".

By the early 1840s there were only seven Presbyterian churches serving about 300 worshippers in south west North Carolina. In comparison 37 Baptist and 32 Methodist congregations were functioning.

The Bethel Presbyterian Church was organised on August 10, 1834 by the Concord Presbytery and given the name Ebenezer Presbyterian Church. The Rev. William A. Hall and Rev. James E. Morrison were in charge of the organisation at a time of the "great removal" of the Cherokee Indians from the region. Ebenezer was under the Morganton Presbytery during the existence of the Presbytery from 1835 to 1840, then it reverted to Concord Presbytery. In 1853 Concord Presbytery changed the name from Ebenezer to Bethel Presbyterian Church.

Mecklenburg Presbytery was formed in 1869 out of the western section of Concord Presbytery, covering the area from Charlotte to Tennessee. Bethel was then transferred to Mecklenburg Presbytery and became a landmark in Haywood County. It was the first Presbyterian church in the county.

For many years the congregation met in Union Meeting House along with Methodists and Baptists. The first church house was erected in

1885 and in 1888 the church building was dedicated by Dr. Sam Boggs of Kentucky. In 1896 Bethel was transferred to Asheville Presbytery when it was formed out of the western portion of Mecklenburg Presbytery. Bethel was the fourth church to be organised in Western North Carolina, being preceded only by Swannanoa, the first in 1794, then Asheville and Davidson River. Other churches were formed at Hayesville, Hendersonsville, Mills River, Oak Forest, Waynesville and Bryson City, the first 10 Presbyterian churches in western North Carolina.

In the 1890s 11 counties west of the Blue Ridge were the neglected backyard of Mecklenburg Presbytery. Although the oldest Presbyterian churches in the region were already a century old, congregations were generally small and weak. Great distances and poor roads meant that western congregations were rarely represented in Presbytery meetings. Illiteracy and ignorance was a feature of these the remote areas.

Some saw great opportunities as well as great needs in the situation. At the urging of R.F. Campbell, pastor of First Presbyterian Church, Asheville; R.P. Smith, Home Missions superintendent; and others, a new presbytery was created in 1896 to include 19 churches, 10 ministers and 1,000 communicant members. The new presbytery brought new life to Presbyterianism in the mountains. By 1909 there were 30 churches, membership had doubled, and many outpost Sunday schools and preaching points were established. Several day schools also opened, and in 1904 the Presbytery founded the first orphanage in the southern Appalachians, now known as the Presbyterian home for children in Black Mountain. By 1926, Asheville Presbytery had 31 churches, 25 ministers and 4,000 members. Membership had increased at a rate three times higher than that of the denomination as a whole. Growth slowed and budgets were cut during the Great Depression, but substantial growth again took place in the years following World War Two. New churches were organised in suburban Asheville and in smaller towns, and membership reached 8,000 in 1958.

Racial tensions caused problems even in Presbyterian church circles in the Carolinas and these became more acute in the years that preceded and during the American Civil War. About 1865 three white Presbyterian ministers, Reverends Samuel C. Alexander, Sidney

Murkland and Willis L. Miller – became disillusioned with the attitude of the Southern Presbyterian Church towards its black members, and gave up their pastorates of white churches to work with the coloured population. The three organised the Catawba Presbytery on October 6, 1866 in the Bethany Church, Iredell County, North Carolina.

The fact that there did not exist synods in the South under the jurisdiction of the General Assembly, U.S.A., the infant presbytery was attached to the Synod of Baltimore. It remained a part of this Synod until 1869, when the Synod of the Atlantic was organised and all the black churches in the South were placed under its jurisdiction. In 1887 the go-ahead was given for the organisation of the Catawba Synod, and twinning existed with three other black Presbyteries in North Carolina and Virginia.

In the years that followed, churches, most of which had schools attached to them, were organised in the surrounding towns and counties. Typical of the developing life in this Presbytery was the founding of four churches in Cabarrus County, organised early in 1867, when the Rev. Luke Dorland gave up his pastorate at the Rocky River Presbyterian Church near Concord to work with black families in the area. The Rev. Dorland saw the need to upgrade the education of black women and organised Scotia Seminary in 1867. Scotia Seminary later merged with Barber College to become what is presently Barber-Scotia College. Today the Catawba Presbytery consists of 31 churches, located in eight counties with just over 5,000 members.

> *"The Scotch-Irish had a system of religious faith and worship which has ever borne an inflexible illusion and mendacity, and has preferred rather to be ground to powder like flint than to bend before violence or melt under enervating temptation."*
> 19th Century Historian, J. A. Froude

28

Ulster victims *of the potato famine*

The horrendous potato famine of the 1840s in Ireland forced a number of Presbyterian families in the small East Antrim village of Raloo near Larne to emigrate. Most of them made it to the Abbeville region of South Carolina, formerly known as "Old 96".

Knox, Blair, Crawford and Evans were among the families who sailed into Charleston in 1844 and, after travelling by train to Augusta, Georgia, they reached the South Carolina back country of Abbeville in covered wagons. The influence of these families in this part of South Carolina over the past 150 years was considerable.

Jeanette (Jenny) Moore Knox came to America with 11 of her 12 children after her blacksmith husband David died in 1840. The extreme hardships endured through the famine had taken a terrible toll, but the Knox family had set their horizons on a new life. When they reached Abbeville the sons and daughters spread out with their families and Jenny lived near Abbeville village with her youngest children.

Her eldest son James left to fight in the Mexican War and never returned, presumed dead. David, married to Nancy Blair, and William, married to Rachel Russell, followed their father's trade as blacksmiths, while Nathaniel and Samuel ended as Confederate soldiers in the Civil War, Nathaniel dying at the Battle of Gaines Mill and Samuel at the Battle of Malvern Hill, both on Virginian soil.

David Crawford Knox, eldest son of David and Nancy Blair Knox, also served as a rifleman in the Civil War and was injured and he too carried on the blacksmith trade in both South Carolina and Georgia. The family were members of Lebanon Presbyterian Church in Abbeville. Back in Co. Antrim they had belonged to Larne and Kilwaughter Presbyterian Churches.

William and Isabelle Locke Evans and their young family of three daughters and a son joined the exodus from Raloo in the early 1840s and headed with other Ulster immigrants to the Lebanon section of Abbeville County. William died in 1847 at the age of 34, making life very difficult for his wife and children. Son James served as a Confederate Cavalryman in the Civil War.

LETTER FROM HOME

A letter written on October 10, 1848 by Samuel and Esther Crawford Blair of Ballyvallough near Larne in Co. Antrim to their daughter Nancy Blair Knox, the wife of David Knox makes interesting reading. It conveys attitudes of the period:

"We are all well and thank God for his kind mercies to us. Hoping this will find you all enjoying the same blessing. We record your kind letter of August 13th, one month after its date. We record no other since McErson arrived with you, if you wrote, it did not come to hand. You say you got your blankets burned. You may expect them to be replenished when Hugh Alexander arrives with you. Be thankful of your children was not burned with the blankets and be kind to the black man who saved the children. Although his skin is black, he is one of God's creations as well as you. Although he is now in bondage, death will set him free.

"We have not heard from John for three years nearly. Write to him when you receive this and let him know his mother is fretting about word from him – thinks he is dead or something wrong with him. Tell him in a few years he will have no father nor mother to write to for we are bending hard towards the grave. We are about 65 years old both born in one year, the both tolerably healthy. We want to know if you have saved any money and how much, and how many cows you have, and what furniture you have in the house, and if you have plenty of work, and how much you earn weekly, the size of your house and how you generally eat and how much you drink of whiskey.

"We have not heard from Samuel for two years nearly. Crawford was with us on Mount Fair Day last, the first of this month. They are all well, Ann and the family are well. She has got another son. Patrick's family is well, only the mistress Esther – she is not well since Mount Hill fair. The fair was on Monday. Ned and her went to Belfast for whiskey on Thursday night – did not get home till Saturday night. Esther over ate herself or got a surfeit or something else did not agree with her and has been in bed ever since. The feeding of Ned has brought her to beggary, he is as ill to feed as an elephant.

"The potato rot has visited us again. 3/4 of the potatoes is rotting out, but hay is abundant. Oat meal is 12 shillings for hundred, potatoes 6 pence, jar stone butter 8 1/2 per pound. Money scarce, trade bad. The Irish rebellion is at an end. Smith O'Brien, their leader, is looking bad and is to die. William Blair of Ballyvallough and Martha Rankin is both dead and David Locke a widower. No more, but may God Almighty protect you and your family. This is the sincere wish of your ever affectionate father and mother till death, Esther and Samuel Blair."

NOTE: There are 112 pounds in one hundred weight, a stone is 14 pounds, a shilling is a five pence or nickel, and a farthing is 1/4 pence. Nancy Blair was the daughter of Samuel Blair and Esther Crawford Blair. Mention of her brothers, who have not written home for some time, refer to John Blair and Samuel Blair.

Builders *of special skills*

Scots-Irish settlers greatly distinguished themselves in many fields, including the building trade, and two Ulstermen with very special talents in this direction were James Dinsmore and John Neilson. Both these master builders who became naturalised citizens of Pennsylvania after their arrival from their Ulster homeland in the late 18th century worked closely with America's third President, Thomas Jefferson, in shaping the landscape of Virginia.

Jefferson, the son of an English colonial planter, was responsible for the Roman paradigm architecture of the immediate post-colonial period in his native Virginia and Dinsmore and Neilson were the craftsmen who plied the skills.

James Dinsmore, born in the Belfast area about 1771, emigrated to America as a young man in his twenties and soon his reputation as a builder was brought to the notice of Thomas Jefferson. Dinsmore's tools were purchased in Philadelphia in 1798, at Jefferson's expense and he was recruited as a master carpenter at the Jefferson estate at Monticello near Charlottsville in the Shenandoah Valley of Virginia. There, Dinsmore was joined by John Neilson, another Belfast-born emigrant, and they set about erecting buildings which were noted for their classical architectural style, among them the University of Virginia at Charlottsville with its distinctive dome and pillared frontage. Later, both men worked for James Monroe, another Virginian and the American President.

29

The best Carolina *cultural and musical tradition*

Celebrated American country music entertainer Clayton McMichen was descended from a Scots-Irish family who settled at Spartanburg in South Carolina in the late 18th century. Georgia-born McMichen was one of the leading personalities in the bluegrass music scene during the early part of this century and was a contemporary of Jimmie Rodgers, A.P. and Maybelle Carter, Bill Monroe and Roy Acuff, pioneers of the traditional country styles which evolved to the modern Nashville sounds of today.

The McMichens were among the finest "old-tyme" fiddlers in the Appalachian region and Clayton's prowess as a musician was acclaimed right across the nation. His versatility extended to fiddlin', singing, songwriting, bandleading, and as a comedian. He was one of Gid Tanner's Skillet Lickers in the 1920s when they made their definitive recording of Wreck of the Old 97 and he regularly appeared at the Grand Ole Opry (the old Ryman Auditorium) in Nashville. Many of the fiddle tunes Clayton and members of his family grew up with were brought to America from the north of Ireland and Scotland: others emerged through the decades from the harsh lifestyles of folk in the Appalachian region.

The first known ancestor of Clayton McMichen in America was John Hiram McMichen, who was born in Spartanburg, South Carolina in 1805. His family left Ireland in the late 18th century and he married Jane Armstrong, who was born in Drung, Co. Cavan, Ireland in 1814.

Jane had come to America with her parents James and Mary, and a brother, in 1825. Another brother was born at sea, on the way over.

The family was originally Presbyterian, some became Methodists, but most joined with the fundamentalist Universalist Church. John Hiram and Jane McMichen moved to Georgia and it is from this line that Clayton was born in 1900. He died in 1970. During the Civil War, the McMichen home in Paulding County, Georgia was used as a Confederate hospital and members of the family saw active service in defence of the Southern cause.

MY CAROLINA HOME
(waltz song)

I've been so lonely since I left my home,
All for you, I know you are waiting
I love you true, I'll never leave Car-o-lin-a again
My old home, there dear I'll always linger
Never again will I roam
For, way down there in Car-o-lin-a, there's where I long to be,
There's where she is waiting, 'neath the old pine tree,
I can hear those mountains calling – come to your mountain home,
Back to your Thelma, and your Car-o-lin-a home.

Days are so long and the nights are so short,
When a-way – thinking about you dear,
I can't say – I keep regretting the time that I left,
My old home – I will promise you dear,
Never a'gain will I roam,
For, way down there in Car-o-lin-a, there's where I long to be,
There's where she's waiting, 'neath the old pine tree,
I can hear those mountains calling,
Come to your mountain home,
Back to your Thelma and your Car-o-lin-a home.

Words and music by Clayton McMichen, Bert Layne
and Lowe Stokes.

MUSIC IN THE WAXHAWS AND HIGHLANDS

The folklore and oral tradition of the Carolina back-country today runs deep into the red clay hills and hollers of what was once the edge of American civilisation, historian and singer/songwriter Karen G. Helms observes.

Union County in North Carolina was settled by Scots-Irish families from the late 1740s and, as the townships grew up, this rich fertile land became known as "the Garden of the Waxhaws". Cotton was grown on some of the farms, but the mixed farming patterns of the Scots-Irish communities were a main feature and a distinct culture grew up around them.

"Most of the folksongs retained from the oral tradition in this region feature humour as an element of relief and a moment of frivolity amidst a work-orientated farm atmosphere. Many of the peoples of Carolina Piedmont have maintained a certain amount of isolation and privacy and this is reflected in the songs that have been handed down over two and a half centuries," says Karen Helms.

This view is echoed by Flora MacDonald Gammon from Waynesville in North Carolina, who enthusiastically maintains the Scottish musical tradition in the Appalachian region through her concert performances and recordings. "Music is the defining expression of the Scots-Irish and Scottish culture in the western highlands of North Carolina. The songs that were handed down from the settlers who came here 200 years ago are still as relevant today for many folk as they were then," she says.

•••

The superstitious and folk beliefs of the Carolina rural up-country people are many and varied. They include:

- For every August fog, there will be a snow in winter.
- Eat the last biscuit on the plate so it will be fair weather tomorrow.
- If your right hand itches, you will meet a stranger; if your left hand itches, you will come into some money.
- A cricket in the house is good luck; to kill one is bad

luck.
• If you sweep under a person's feet, he (she) will never marry.
• If you dream of snow, someone you know will die soon.
• Heavy amounts of red berries on piracantha bushes mean an unusually hard winter.
• Kiss a red-haired person to cure fever blisters.
• Dig post holes by the light of the moon and the posts will set in as if in concrete.
• To enter one door and exit another is bad luck.
• To stop a chain of infant deaths, name the next male child Adam, the next female Eve.

•••

Medicine remedies still practiced in the Waxhaws region, are:

• For kidney trouble, boil some staghorn in a pot and drink the tea or just chew up the sour red berries of the plant.
• For earache, take a piece of hair from another race, place it in your ear and pain will disappear.
• To cure warts, take a half of an Irish potato, rub on the warts, bury the potato and when it rots the warts will be gone.
• For a sprain, take a dirt dobber's nest and mix with vinegar and place this around the sprain, secured with an old rag.
• Use soot and spider webs to stop bleeding.
• Catch the first snow of the year, melt this and use on burns throughout the year. Helps in healing and prevents scars.
• To cure sores on the hand, let a dog lick the wound.
• To cure a bad cold, boil green pine straw and put it in a little sugar. Drink this as a tea.
• An axe under the bed will help cut labour pains.

30

Co. Down colonies *in Virginia and South Carolina*

Presbyterian families from Banbridge in Co. Down were at the original settlement at Opequon near Winchester at the north east rim of the Shenandoah Valley of Virginia. This rural township was settled in the 1730s by immigrants who had just arrived in from Ulster and the (simple) Presbyterian meeting house was the corner-stone of the community. It was the oldest church west of the Blue Ridge Mountains.

The Opequon settlement took its name from Opequon Creek and River, a tributary of the Potomac which flowed north along the centre of the lower Shenandoah Valley. There, Samuel Glass, from Banbridge was among the first Europeans to settle and his grandson, historian the Rev. William Henry Foote, gives a full account of his company.

"Samuel Glass took up residence at the head-spring of the Opequon, and his neighbours were son-in-law John Becket, son Robert, Joseph Colvin and family, John Wilson and the Marquis family, the McAuleys, William Hoge, the Allen family, Robert Wilson and James Vance. They were all here as early as 1736 or 1737. Other families gathered around these in a country abounding with prairie and pea vines, and buffalo and deer."

Alongside the Co. Down families were German settlers, who, like the Ulster folk, had entered the region from Pennsylvania. Samuel Glass and his group landed in Philadelphia and acquired land through German immigrant Jost Hite, who was land agent for Lord Fairfax.

The average farm in the Opequon region was 150 acres, with the settlers mainly into grain (wheat, rye, oats, barley, buckwheat and corn) and livestock (cattle, horses, sheep and swine). Hemp, flax and tobacco were also grown.

The Opequon Presbyterian settlement was a closely defined community, the men aged 25 to 50 travelling from Banbridge, Co. Down with their families intact. Family, kin, ethnicity and land binded the Scots-Irish community at Opequon and in one of the first collective acts they established a Presbyterian congregation and erected a church. As early as 1735, Opequon settlers invited the Rev. Samuel Gelston, a member of the Donegal Presbytery in Pennsylvania, to preach and the following year he was appointed in charge. Samuel Glass was a trustee of the church.

By 1745, the population of Opequon had grown considerably – it was 4,300 in the surrounding Frederick County – and while there was large influx of newcomers, significantly the 10 families of the first generation produced a total offspring of 50. Land was passed on through the families but after several generations when tracts became scarce, younger members moved to the new territories opening up in Kentucky, Tennessee and Ohio.

As William Henry Foote observed in his sketches of Virginia: "Reports from the west painted Kentucky as more beautiful in its solitariness than Opequon had been to the eyes of the emigrants from Ireland". Eighteen members of the third generation of the family of Samuel Glass left for Kentucky as the covered wagons rolled to open up the frontier beyond the Allegheny Mountains.

Just as Northern Ireland has its town of Newry in Co. Down, so too has South Carolina a Newry. This quiet sleepy township, which lies 30 miles west of Greenville in the foothills of the Great Smoky Mountains, has a population of around 3,000 and grew up around the plantation of Captain William Ashmead Courtenay, Mayor of Charleston for eight years in the 1880s. The Courtenays were an Irish family of substance and it was Edward Courtenay who settled in South Carolina in 1791 after arriving at Charleston from his home at Newry in Ulster.

Newry in Co. Down has a population of 25,000 and in 1994 when the town marked its 800th anniversary, residents from Newry, South Carolina travelled across for the celebrations. There is also a Newry township in Pennsylvania.

William Ashmead Courtenay was in the publishing and bookselling business in Charleston and when the Civil War broke out he joined the Confederate Army. He served as a Captain with the Washington Light Infantry.

In April, 1893 Courtenay was authorised to establish a factory for the manufacture of cotton and wool and this was sited on 300 acres in the north west corner of South Carolina close to Georgia, North Carolina and Tennessee. The mill village was named Newry after his family's home town in Ulster and it proved an ideal site with ample water supplies for the factory from the Little River.

At its height, the Courtenay mill provided work for 120 people and in the early 1900s Newry had a school, church, company store, post office, meat market and barber's shop. Captain William Ashmeade Courtenay ran the business with his son Campbell, but in 1920 the property and stock was sold to Issaqueena Mills of South Carolina. The mill, sadly, closed its doors in April, 1975 after the textile industry went into world recession.

Today, the spacious Courtenay mill at Newry lies derelict and the village is without any form of industry, except small farm holdings. Remaining residents of employment age commute to neighbouring towns like Clemson and Seneca for work. All that is left in Newry is the post office and general store with Baptist, Methodist and Pentecostal churches dotted along its three main streets.

Newry, in its heyday was a typical, thriving South Carolina mill village established by an entrepreneurial Ulster family who found the warm southern climate ideally suited for their industry.

An American view *of the Scots-Irish*
by Bil Gilbert

"Perhaps no other sizable group of emigrants arrived in North America with less baggage, material or culture, than did the Scotch-Irish. Because of poverty and insecurity, they had acquired few traditional folkways, arts or crafts and almost none they cared enough about to try to bring with them and transplant in the New World. Presbyterianism was one of their few possessions of this sort, but it did not do well in the wilds of North America. Some of the emigrants held to the kirks, but more turned to exotic native frontier churches or simply decided that religion of any sort was unnecessary and frivolous in the wilderness. This, too, turned out to be of adaptive benefit for the Scotch-Irish. They wasted little effort trying to recreate European villages, schools, gardens, farms, trades, diets, fashions or social customs. Without nostalgic regret they accepted the reality that they were in a new place where European experience counted for little and could be largely ignored."

• **BIL GILBERT is an award-winning American journalist and author of The Trailblazers and Westering Man (The Life of Joseph Walker), books on the exploration of western North America.**

Author's *acknowledgments*

- President Jimmy Carter, Atlanta, Georgia.
- John Rice Irwin, Museum of Appalachia, Norris, Tennessee.
- H. David Wright (Artist), Nashville, Tennessee.
- Alister McReynolds, Principal, Lisburn College, Co. Antrim.
- Thomas Moore Craig Jun., Roebuck, Spartanburg County, South Carolina.
- Lynn R. McR. Hawkins, Bluff City, Tennessee.
- Barbara Parker, Department of Tourist Development, Nashville, Tennessee.
- Dr. Ian Adamson, former Lord Mayor of Belfast.
- Flora MacDonald Gammon, Waynesville, North Carolina.
- Robert Anderson (Printer), Richhill, Co. Armagh.
- Geoff Martin, Editor Ulster News Letter, Belfast.
- Dr. Bobby Gilmer Moss, Blacksburg, South Carolina.
- Dr. Thomas W. Burton, formerly East Tennessee State University.
- Cherel Henderson, East Tennessee Historical Society, Knoxville.
- Will Hiott and Leslie Nelson, Fort Hill University, Clemson, South Carolina.
- Stevan Jackson, Director Appalachian-Scottish Studies, East Tennessee State University.
- Karen G. Helms, Wingate University, North Carolina.
- Robert O. King, Greenville, South Carolina.
- Ralph P. Ganis, Director, Andrew Jackson Museum, Waxhaw, Charlotte, North Carolina.
- Councillor George Shiels, Maghera, Co. Londonderry.
- Tommy Rye, Maryville, Blount County, Tennessee.
- Dr. Katharine Brown, Museum of American Frontier Culture, Staunton, Virginia.
- Jane Wilson, Donalds Historical Society, South Carolina.
- Elsie Hammond, Caldwell Fields, Pomaria, South Carolina.
- Bob Hamilton (Photographer), Ulster/Belfast News Letter.
- Teri Penik, Administrator, Walnut Grove Plantation, Roebuck, South Carolina.
- C. Allen Coleman, Curator, County of Pickens Museum, South Carolina.

- Harry Sandlin, Bob Jones University, Greenville, South Carolina.
- Dr. Daniel Byron Verdin Jun., Greenville, South Carolina.
- Terry Rude, Bob Jones University, Greenville, South Carolina.
- George Hamilton IV, Franklin, Tennessee.
- Elsie Greene Wilcox, Monroe, North Carolina.
- Susie K. New, Abbeville, South Carolina.
- Ralph R. Parke, Edgewood, Kentucky.
- Richard McMaster, Pennsylvania.
- C. Newell Bowie, Due West, South Carolina.
- Nancy Knox Schaffer, Kildeer, Illinois.
- Jerome Rankin Wallace, Honolulu, Hawaii.
- Edwin A. Meeks, Jonesborough, Tennessee.
- Evelyn Hanson Helton, Kingsport, Tennessee
- Hal Donnald Sharp, Cornelius, North Carolina.
- Dr. Harry L. Reeder III, Christ Covenant Presbyterian Church, Charlotte, North Carolina.
- Dr. Charles Moffatt, Gallatin, Tennessee.
- Clara J. Mann, Flat Rock, North Carolina.
- John and Carole Lebert, Knoxville, Tennessee.
- J. Farrell Saunders, Superintendent, Cowpens National Battlefield, Chesnee, South Carolina.
- Miller Jun., and Virginia M. Jones, Oak Ridge, Tennessee.
- Dawson H. Hogsed, Pisgah Forest, North Carolina.
- Lavina McKnight Kienast, Kinston, North Carolina.
- Andrew M. Loveless, Superintendent, Kings Mountain National Military Park, North Carolina.
- Ronnie Allen, Carrickfergus, Co. Antrim.
- Eric Williams, Ninety Six Historic Site, South Carolina.
- Stan Hodges, Perry, Oklahoma.
- Chris McIvor, Librarian, Ulster-American Folk Park, Omagh, Co. Tyrone.
- Linda Patterson, Ambassador/Causeway Productions, Belfast.
- Library Staff, Carrickfergus, Co. Antrim.
- Joe Barbee, Library, Salisbury, Rowan County, North Carolina.
- Loretta B. Junkin, Vienna, Virginia.
- Frank Downey, Banbridge Heritage Trail, Co. Down.
- Robert Ashley Logue, Sumner County, Tennessee.
- Colin Baxter, Tandragee, Co. Armagh.
- Professor Michael Montgomery, University of South Carolina, Columbia.
- Edward O. McCue III, Charlottsville, Virginia.
- Colin Magee, North Down Borough Council, Bangor.

Bibliography *and references consulted*

- Carolina Cradle, Settlement of the Northwest Carolina Frontier 1747-62 by Robert W. Ramsey.
- The Carolina Backcountry by Charles Woodmason.
- The Great Wagon Road by Parke Rouse Jun.
- Historic Walnut Grove Plantation 1765.
- Daniel Boone, Master of the Wilderness by John Bakeless.
- Kings Mountain and Its Heroes by Lyman C. Draper.
- The Career of Arthur Dobbs of Carrickfergus 1689-1765.
- The Patriots at Cowpens by Dr. Bobby Gilmer Moss.
- The Patriots at Kings Mountain by Dr. Bobby Gilmer Moss.
- The Scotch-Irish, A Social History by James G. Leyburn.
- Westering Man, the Life of Joseph Walker by Bil Gilbert.
- The Encyclopedia of the South, edited by Robert O'Brien.
- Ulster Emigration to Colonial America 1718-1775 by R.J. Dickson.
- The Complete List of U.S. Presidents by William A. Degregorio.
- Cousin Monroe's History of the Pickens Family.
- The Heritage of Rowan County, North Carolina.
- Patriots, Pistols and Petticoats by Walter J. Fraser Jun.
- South Carolina – The WPA Guide to the Palmetto State.
- History of Rowan County by James S. Brawley.
- A History of Rowan County, North Carolina by Rev. Jethro Rumple.
- History of Davie County, North Carolina by James W. Wall
- The Rowan Story (North Carolina) 1753-1953 by James S. Brawley.
- Ninety Six – The Struggle for the South Carolina Back County by Robert D. Bass.
- South Carolina, A Synoptic History for Laymen by Lewis P. Jones.
- South Carolina – A Short History by David Duncan Wallace.
- History of Spartanburg County by Dr. J.B. O. Landrum.
- Long Rifles of North Carolina by John Bivins Jun.

- Boonesborough Township by C. Newell Bowie.
- The Overmountain Men by Pat Alderman.
- The Wataugans by Max Dixon.
- South Carolina Naturizations 1783-1850 by Brent H. Holcomb.
- Thomas Jefferson and his World by Henry Moscow.
- America's First Western Frontier : East Tennessee by Brenda C. Calloway.
- History of the Lost State of Franklin by Samuel Cole-Williams.
- The Highland Scots of North Carolina 1732-76 by Duane Meyer.
- The Frontier Rifleman by Richard B. Lacrosse Jun.
- Scotch-Irish Migration to South Carolina 1772 by Jean Stephenson.
- History of the Presbyterian Church in South Carolina by George Howe.
- Dictionary of American Regional English (Volume 1)
- From Ulster to Carolina by Tyler Blethen and Curtis Wood Jun.
- The Road to Guilford Courthouse (The American Revolution in the Carolinas) by John Buchanan.
- Charles Thomson, "Prime Minister" of the United States by Fred S. Rolater.
- Harriton of Bryn Mawr, Pennsylvania.
- Charles Thomson, Secretary of Congress 1774-1789 by Kenneth R. Bowling.
- The Great Seal of the United States (published by the US Department of State, July 1980)
- Masters Family History 1691-1989.
- History of Nazareth Presbyterian Church, Moore, South Carolina.
- Hand--Me-Down Songs (Traditional Music of North Carolina) by Karen G. Helms.
- Belfast News Letters, 250 Years (1737-1987).
- Stories of the Great West by President Theodore Roosevelt.
- The Highest Call by Ronnie Hanna, Ulster Society.
- With Fire and Sword by Wilma Dykeman.
- Land of the Free; Ulster and the American Revolution – Ronnie Hanna, Ulster Society.
- The Mecklenburg Declaration of Independence by George W. Graham.
- Leave-Taking – The Scotch-Irish Come to Western North Carolina by H. Tyler Blethern Curtis Wood Jun.
- Andrew Pickens (Oconee County Historical Society, North Carolina).
- Greenville Presbyterian Church, Donalds Presbyterian Church: Church Cemetery and Genealogical Data.
- Andrew Jackson's Hermitage.
- Kate Barry by Mary Montgomery Miller.
- The Bayonets at Fort Ligonier, Pennsylvania 1758-1766 by Joseph R. Marsden.
- Centenial History of First Associate Reformed Presbyterian Church, Rock Hill, South Carolina by Paul M. Gettys.
- Greenville – The History of City and Country in the South Carolina Piedmont.
- History of Fairview Presbyterian Church by Mary Lou Stewart Garrett
- The Hearst Family - the early years.

Pictures *and illustrations*

- H. David Wright (Artist), Nashville.
- Hudson Studio, Greenville, South Carolina.
- Carrickfergus and District Historical Society, Co. Antrim.
- Ralph P. Ganis, Director, Andrew Jackson Museum, Waxhaw, North Carolina.
- Ulster Belfast/News Letter.
- David Scott, Maghera, Co. Londonderry.
- Fort Hill University, Clemson, South Carolina.
- Eric Williams, Ninety Six Historic Site, South Carolina.
- Robert O. King, Greenville, South Carolina.
- Northern Ireland Tourist Board.
- Bob Hamilton, Ulster/Belfast News Letter.
- Jane Wilson, Donnalds Historical Society.
- Dr. Charles L. Moffatt, Gallatin, Tennessee.
- Councillor George Shiels, Maghera, Co. Londonderry.
- Robert Windsor Wilson.
- David Scott, Maghera, Co. Londonderry.

Presidents of the United States

Order	Name	Party	Age at Inaug.	State Where Born	Age at Death
1	George Washington	Fed.	57	VA	67
2	John Adams	Fed.	61	MA	90
3	Thomas Jefferson	Dem.-Rep.	57	VA	83
4	James Madison	Dem.-Rep.	57	VA	73
5	James Monroe	Dem.-Rep.	58	VA	73
6	John Quincy Adams	Dem.-Rep.	57	MA	80
7	Andrew Jackson	Dem.	61	SC	78
8	Martin Van Buren	Dem.	54	NY	79
9	William Henry Harrison	Whig	68	VA	68
10	John Tyler	Whig	51	VA	71
11	James Knox Polk	Dem.	49	NC	53
12	Zachary Taylor	Whig	64	VA	65
13	Millard Fillmore	Whig	50	NY	74
14	Franklin Pierce	Dem.	48	NH	64
15	James Buchanan	Dem.	65	PA	77
16	Abraham Lincoln	Rep.	52	KY	56
17	Andrew Johnson	Dem.-Rep.	56	NC	66
18	Ulysses Simpson Grant	Rep.	46	OH	63
19	Rutherford Birchard Hayes	Rep.	54	OH	70
20	James Abram Garfield	Rep.	49	OH	49
21	Chester Alan Arthur	Rep.	50	VT	56
22	Grover Cleveland	Dem.	47	NJ	71
23	Benjamin Harrison	Rep.	55	OH	67
24	Grover Cleveland	Dem.	55	NJ	71
25	William McKinley	Rep.	54	OH	58
26	Theodore Roosevelt	Rep.	42	NY	60
27	William Howard Taft	Rep.	51	OH	72
28	Woodrow Wilson	Dem.	56	VA	67
29	Warren Gamaliel Harding	Rep.	55	OH	57
30	Calvin Coolidge	Rep.	51	VT	60
31	Herbert Clark Hoover	Rep.	54	IA	90
32	Franklin Delano Roosevelt	Dem.	51	NY	63
33	Harry S. Truman	Dem.	60	MO	88
34	Dwight David Eisenhower	Rep.	62	TX	78
35	John Fitzgerald Kennedy	Dem.	43	MA	46
36	Lyndon Baines Johnson	Dem.	55	TX	64
37	Richard Milhous Nixon	Rep.	56	CA	81
38	Gerald Rudolph Ford	Rep.	61	NE	-
39	James Earl Carter Jr.	Dem.	52	GA	-
40	Ronald Wilson Reagan	Rep.	69	IL	-
41	George Herbert Walker Bush	Rep.	65	MA	-
42	William Jefferson Clinton	Dem.	47	AR	-

Index

Mc

McArdle, Eliza 42
McAden, Rev. Hugh 106
McAdow, Rev. Samuel 97
McBride, Rev. Alexander 30
McCorkle - Alexander 96, Dr. Samuel
Eusebius 96, 106, 107
McDonald - John 65, Hugh 65-66,
William 66
McClintock - Rev. Robert 60, Timothy
60, John 60
McDowell, William 47
McDill, Thomas 63
McCalla - David 66, Thomas 66
McClure, Matthew 130
McGarity, William 66
McGee, Rev. William 97
McMichen - Clyaton 187-188, John
Hiram 187, 188, Jane Armstrong 187-
188
McKown - Alexander 66, James 66,
John 66, Moses 66
McClurken - Thomas 60, John 60,
John 66, Matthew 66, Thomas 66
McCosh, Rev. John 84
McCulloh, Henry 100
McKinley, President William 48
McElrath, John 86
McKeen, James 30
McKeown, Alexander 65
McKean, Thomas 131
McGarragh, Rev. James 64
McClurkin, James 170
McLurkin, James 62
McLurken, Richard 62
McClenaghan, John 62
McNeel, Archibald 62
MacGregar, Rev. James 29-30
McVicker (McVickar) 58-59
McReynolds - Alister J. 13-16, Andrew
Thomas 14
McQuestin - David 62-63, James 62
McWilliams, Archibald 62
McQuillan, John 62

McGinley - Colonel James 170-171,
William Dunwoody 171
McWaters, John 66
McWhorter - Rev. Alexander 106,

M

Madill, Thomas 60
Martin - David 57, John 66, Rev.
William 33, 57, 58, 61, 62, 63, 64, 65,
66, 92, 125, 171, Mary 65, Jenny 65,
Susanna 65, Sarah Dunn 66, David 174
Makee, Thomas 60
Mackemie, Rev. Francis 12
Mayes, Dr. Samuel 74
Mansoad, Hugh 60
Machesney, Robert 60
Menary, Gilbert 62
Miller - Charles 60, 62, Samuel 62,
William 62, John 155, Willis L. 182
Millar, James 158
Mitchell John 30, Joab 156
Moffatt - William 65, 125, Barbara
Chestnut 65, 125
Mophet, Samuel 65
Moore - Charles 77, 78, 79, 82. William
77, Mary Barry 77, 79, 82, Andrew 78,
79, Thomas 79, 80, 87, Charles Jun. 79,
Alice 79, Rosa 79, 80, Rachel 79, Violet
79, Elizabeth 79, John 58, Colonel
Thomas John 82
Morrison - John 30, William S. 44,
William 96, James E. 180, John 171,
172, 174, William 173, Nancy 173,
Archibald 171, Elizabeth 171, 174,
Daniel 171, 172, 173, 174
Monroe, President James 89, 186
Morgan, General Daniel 80
Moss, Dr. Bobby Gilmer 153-158
Montgomery - John 58-60, David 62
Murrray - Captain Adam 29, David 62
Murkland, Sydney 182

THE SCOTS-IRISH CHRONICLES
By Billy Kennedy

The Scots-Irish in the Hills of Tennessee
(First Published 1995)

Centred in Tennessee, this is the absorbing story about a race of people who created a civilisation in a wilderness and helped lay the sole foundations for what today is the greatest nation on earth. The Scots-Irish Presbyterians who settled in the American frontier during the 18th century were a unique breed of people with an independent spirit which boldly challeged the arbitrary powers of monarchs and established church prelates.

The battles with the British forces, the native American tribes and the elements in a climate that had its extremes, took a terrible toll on the men, women and children, but with a doggedness and steely character inherent in their culture, the brave Scots-Irish pioneers won through.

The book records for prosterity the daring exploits of a people who tamed the frontier. It is a story that needs to be told, retold and told over and over again so that the light of democracy and freedom can shine brightly in the complex world in which we live.

The Scots-Irish in the Shenandoah Valley
(First Published 1996)

The beautiful Shenandoah Valley alongside the majestic backdrop of the Blue Ridge Mountains of Virginia is the idyllic setting for the intriguing story of a resolute people who tamed the wilderness of the American frontier. The Ulster Presbyterian stock, or the Scots-Irish, as they were known, created a civilisation in the Shenandoah during the 18th century that was to be the springboard for further frontier advance and settlement to the west.

In the Shenandoah Valley, the Scots-Irish were real achievers and leaders in their community, church and state. American President Woodrow Wilson came of this ilk; so too did distinguished American Civil War generals Thomas Jonathan "Stonewall" Jackson and J.E.B. Stuart; innovative farm reaper inventor Cyrus McCormick; celebrated author Mark Twain (Clemens), and soldier/statesman General Sam Houston, the Governor of Texas and Tennessee.

The Ulster-Scots were a breed of people who could move mountains. They did this literally with their bare hands 200 years ago, winning the day for freedom and liberty of conscience in the United States.

*Available in hardback and softback from booksellers or
direct from the publisher (see address on page 2).*